C000102178

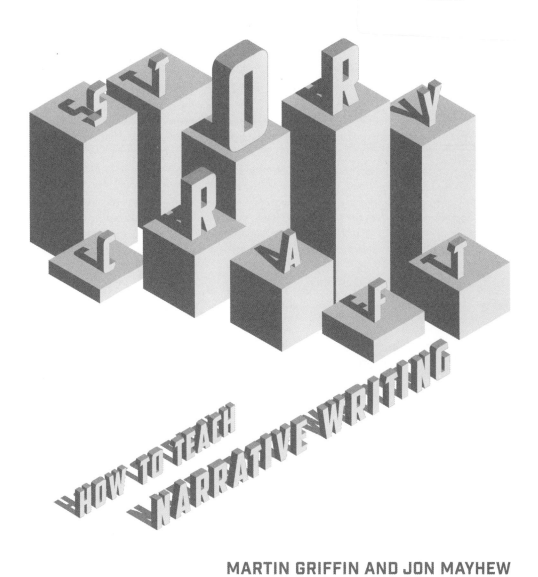

HOW TO TEACH NARRATIVE WRITING

MARTIN GRIFFIN AND JON MAYHEW

Crown House Publishing Limited
www.crownhouse.co.uk

First published by
Crown House Publishing
Crown Buildings, Bancyfelin, Carmarthen, Wales, SA33 5ND, UK
www.crownhouse.co.uk

and

Crown House Publishing Company LLC
PO Box 2223, Williston, VT 05495, USA
www.crownhousepublishing.com

© Martin Griffin and Jon Mayhew, 2019

The rights of Martin Griffin and Jon Mayhew to be identified as the authors of this work have been asserted by them in accordance with the Copyright, Designs and Patents Act 1988.

First published 2019.

Illustration p. 15 © Les Evans, 2019.

Cover images © LiliGraphie, L.Dep – fotolia.com

All rights reserved. Except as permitted under current legislation no part of this work may be photocopied, stored in a retrieval system, published, performed in public, adapted, broadcast, transmitted, recorded or reproduced in any form or by any means, without the prior permission of the copyright owners. Enquiries should be addressed to Crown House Publishing.

Quotes from Ofsted and Department for Education documents used in this publication have been approved under an Open Government Licence. Please see: http://www.nationalarchives. gov.uk/doc/open-government-licence/version/3/.

British Library of Cataloguing-in-Publication Data
A catalogue entry for this book is available from the British Library.

LCCN 2019947469

Print ISBN 978-178583402-8
Mobi ISBN 978-178583463-9
ePub ISBN 978-178583464-6
ePDF ISBN 978-178583465-3

Printed in the UK by
Gomer Press, Llandysul, Ceredigion

PREFACE

We've managed to clock up over twenty years each in the classroom as English teachers at Key Stages 3, 4 and 5. In some ways our teaching careers have been very different. Martin began his career in sixth form colleges teaching GCSE English retake courses and English A levels; later he moved to the 11–18 sector. He has been a head of English and deputy head teacher. Jon has taught English in a wide variety of secondary schools – some in leafy suburbs, others in neglected and forgotten housing estates, heading English in special settings and working with some of the most challenging children in the education system.

Despite these differences we've been united in our passion for creative writing. Writing professionally while holding down a teaching career hasn't been easy. We've both had to eke out an hour here and there – mostly late at night – and finish our respective books one painstaking scene at a time. Martin's nine books are split between award-winning fiction (three novels for teenage readers: *The Poison Boy*, *Lifers* and *Payback*) and non-fiction (educational texts on developing metacognition and study skills co-authored with Steve Oakes: *The A Level Mindset*, *The GCSE Mindset* and *The Student Mindset*). Martin's output is dwarfed, however, by Jon's twenty-six novels for children and adults, which include the award-winning *Mortlock* and Monster Odyssey series. Jon's work includes retellings of *Macbeth*, *Romeo and Juliet* and *Hamlet*; high age interest/low reading age books for teens; and articles for various writing and educational publications. He's also been a contributor to the *Children's Writers' and Artists' Yearbook* since 2014.

When we first met and began discussing our respective experiences we were struck by how our regular contact with publishing house editors, with their forensic understanding of story and exacting standards, had begun to inform our teaching. We felt better equipped to teach creative writing because we had been lucky enough to receive very practical tutoring from some of the best editors and publishers in the country.

Since then, our insights have informed our writing workshops and changed the way we intervene, support and give feedback. In his role as Writing Fellow for the Royal Literary Fund at the Universities of Chester and Aberystwyth, Jon even found that the fundamentals of creative writing could be brought to undergraduate academic assignments.

Storycraft is our attempt to share as many of these principles and strategies as we can. This book is by no means a complete curriculum: pick and choose the activities you think will best benefit your students and discard the others.

Stay in touch at www.storycraftbook.com or @Storycraft6 on Twitter.

And whatever your approach, enjoy the process!

ACKNOWLEDGEMENTS

The ideas in this book are the result of years of road testing in high schools all over the country. It takes a lot of faith and trust to hand over an exam class, or even a whole year group, to a wild-eyed author with a suitcase full of half-baked ideas.

Martin would like to thank:

Darren Tyldsley, assistant head teacher at Ellesmere Park, for his support and feedback, and Elaine Perry at The Blue Coat School, who is partly responsible for starting this whole process by finding space in the timetable for an experimental Year 9 creative writing class all those years ago.

Everyone at The Portico Library, Manchester, for their enthusiasm, passion and dedication to narrative writing. Special thanks to all those who help run the superb Sadie Massey Awards for young readers and writers: Lynne Allan, Ruth Estevez, Aoife Larkin and Paul Morris.

Claire Baylis at St Edmund Arrowsmith, Jane Kingsford – happy retirement! – at Bolton School, Irena Savova at St Pauls, Joanne Weightman at Allestree Woodlands, and Gerald Bruen at Lytham High School for arranging repeat visits and tolerating the stress-testing of this and other material as it was being developed.

Jon would like to thank:

Librarians Jane Griffiths at Alsager School and Charlotte Pearson at Neston High School for their support through the years and for allowing him to experiment in workshops.

John Anderson and the English department at Chase Terrace Technology College; Helen Foster, head of English, drama and media studies at Pensby High School; Bev Ivins and Andy Moorcroft at Beamont Collegiate Academy; Paul Pearson, head of English, and Sarah Kirwan, second in department, at Neston High School; and the BOLD cluster of primary schools, Warrington. Also, Steve Cook and David Swinburne at the Royal Literary Fund for giving him the space to breathe, step back and look at what worked and what didn't in his school workshops.

CONTENTS

INTRODUCTION

This book is not about style. It won't give you activities that encourage students to use fronted adverbials, vary their premodification or employ the passive voice. We think there's plenty of that about.

Instead, *Storycraft* focuses on getting students writing – putting words and ideas on paper as regularly and confidently as possible.

Too often we found that our creative writing classes went like this: we'd read and discuss a great piece of writing; we'd stay where we, as teachers, felt most comfortable (analysing the writer's linguistic tricks and enthusing about them); we'd line up a writing task; and then we'd watch as thirty kids seemed unable to summon sufficient energy to put anything on paper. There would be awkward silence. Then the questions would come: 'How do I start?' 'What should happen?' 'What do I write next?' 'Am I allowed to [insert whatever]?' 'Can you give me another word meaning "scared"?' and, inevitably, 'Can I swear?'

And once the work was in, our feedback would be all about style. We'd read thirty stories and make observations like, 'Can you use an inventive simile here?' or scribble, 'Is there a better adjective?' in the margin of the student's piece. But questions of style come much later. Adjustments in wording are the final stage of a much longer process.

This may be the first book we've written together, but we've known each other a long time, and over the years we've had hundreds of hours of telephone conversations with agents and editors as we discussed manuscripts in development. Almost none of that time has been spent on questions of style.

Instead, we've found that editors and publishers want the architecture of the piece to be sorted out first. Under discussion were things like: how can we get the protagonist right? What is driving this character? What do they want? Tell me about motivation in this scene. Why isn't the pace right here? Who do you consider to be the foreground characters? How is this character changing? How does the structure of the novel work? Describe the shape of this story. What is at its heart and how will it end? Only after months and months of writing might we get a read-through with style as a focus.

This book will be about getting students to a point where they've written well enough that we legitimately have the luxury of debating matters of style, rather than beginning there.

Storycraft is about the craft of getting character, setting and structure coherent and strong. There are fifty-one activities that will get your students crafting narratives regularly, more quickly and with gradually greater confidence. The book is about exploring the creative process so that we can normalise the struggles associated with crafting something from nothing.

It might be purchased with a Year 11 class in mind, but this is a set of tools, tricks and strategies that can be used at any level. Try it at Key Stage 3 or with A level students. We still use many of these tricks regularly ourselves.

We've divided the book into seven main sections:

1. In **Manifesto for a Creative Classroom** we explore the creative process. *Process* is a key concept here. Great writing doesn't arrive out of nowhere, no matter what the eureka moment myths and legends might suggest. What goes on in a writer's head as they develop a story? Where do all their good ideas come from? What habits and routines do writers use so they always have good ideas ready to go? What happens before the real writing starts?

    We've tried to codify the process in this chapter of the book. Our FORGE acronym suggests that good creative thinking requires *feeding* (providing the imagination with fuel), followed by *observing* and *researching* (paying active attention to the world with a curiosity that allows us to better represent what we see). *Gestation* is important: the creative process is a long game. The ideas we generate on the morning of a writing exam may be nascent, weak and derivative. Those we have considered critically for longer will have an inherent strength. Finally, *experimentation* will play a role. New and interesting ideas are often nothing more than familiar concepts combined in new ways. We also tackle ten misconceptions about creative writing in this chapter.

2. In **FORGE-ing Strategies** we provide ten activities that help students to generate micro-ideas – the valuable little nuggets that work as seeds for great stories. The activities are written for students and address them directly. You can direct students to them and (hopefully) they will be able to follow the instructions and begin work.

    There are no writing tasks at the end of these activities. FORGE largely describes the pre-production process and results in notes, scribbles, discussion and lists of possibilities. The outcomes of these activities should be captured, shared and discussed; the crafting process comes next.

3. Character is the heart of any good narrative. In **Crafting Characters** we share ten strategies for making characters better. The activities are written for students and address them directly. As before, you can direct students to them and they should be able to follow the instructions and begin work. Unlike the previous chapter, however, these activities require students to be 'ready to write' and to actually get something down on paper. Typically they require students to produce 300–400 words (Why this amount? We've found it works best for us. Five- and six-year-old pupils in Years 2 and 3, writing at length for the first time, can often manage 100 words. We think that seven or eight years later, 300 words is the least we might expect. But we recognise, of course, that this might not be easy, and might not suit your context. Adjust as you see fit!). There are a few helpful bullet points to get them up and running. As their teacher you'll be able to use or ignore these.

4. Narratives don't take place in colourless spaces. Location adds mood, atmosphere and momentum. In **Crafting Settings** we offer ten activities that take us away from the ubiquitous spooky cottage or school canteen. As with the previous chapter, each of the activities are written directly for students. By the end of the resource they should be ready to write, so each activity ends with a writing task of 300–400 words, and, as above, you'll be able to make any adjustments you want.

5. In **Crafting Shape and Structure** we offer ten activities to help students shape their stories. We've tried to go beyond beginning/middle/end, but not to confuse the issue by introducing narratology or structural analysis. We think that a story composed of two or three coherent and well-chosen scenes will be streets ahead of those made up on the fly. As before, the students should work through the activities themselves, at the end of which they should be ready to write around 300–400 words.

6. In **Editing** we offer some solutions to common story problems. We've spoken to English teachers who have been open enough to share student narratives with us. One of the themes that regularly emerges from these discussions is the ease with which we can spot misfiring narratives, but the difficulty we all have in pinpointing the exact problem with them. 'I know these are weak,' one teacher said to us as we read through student pieces. 'But *why* are they weak?' The activities in this chapter are designed to diagnose and improve already existing pieces. As such, there are no writing activities at the end of these resources. They only work if the student brings an already completed piece of writing to them.

7. Finally, in **The Exam** we offer five tips for exam preparation written directly for students and with an impending creative writing exam in mind.

We end with Activity 51: there are thirty-nine writing prompts to round off the book, one for each week of the academic year. We hope you find them useful!

CHAPTER 1

MANIFESTO FOR A CREATIVE CLASSROOM

If you search the internet for 'the scientific method' you get, at the time of writing, over 17 million hits, including Wikipedia pages, articles, definitions, images, beginner's guides and introductions for various key stages.

If you search the internet for 'the creative method' you get fewer than 300,000 hits; that's 1.76% of the pages dedicated to the scientific method. (The Creative Method, we discovered, is also the name of a Sydney-based design agency.)

Why the disparity? The characteristics of the scientific method have been established for nearly 500 years. You have a hypothesis which generates logical predictions. You then test these and gather evidence. The experiment must be replicable and peer approved. You arrive at a greater understanding having deconstructed something.

Scientific classrooms have the equipment and tools necessary to make these analyses. They have a lab assistant who wheels in trolleys of jars and test tubes from a stock-room full of materials. They have posters illustrating cross-section cutaways of hearts and eyes, drawings of light bouncing off surfaces, lists of parts and components.

But the creative method is about construction, not deconstruction. Moving from having nothing to having something you have crafted and built.

There is much discussion about how this process works, and every creative seems to be doing something very different. The picture is complicated by the fact that some writers and artists aren't sure where their ideas come from and ascribe spiritual significance to them. Others claim to 'hear voices' or explain that all we have to do is 'unearth the story'. Others speak of sudden flashes of inspiration.

All of this makes it harder to conceive of a 'creative writing classroom'. Although it's tempting to conjure up ideas of bright colours, informal seating, fun activities and eureka moments, these notions do nothing to encourage creative output. We've been teaching and writing for a combined forty years and when we sit at home to create we're typing at a desk, alone. We're responding to a brief having signed a contract for a book which specifies the length, audience, probable title and content. We're on a deadline and we've got daily word count targets to reach.

Our manifesto for a creative classroom is an attempt to organise and formalise everything we've learned about the creative process. There are no weird or wacky suggestions here – nothing about sitting on a beanbag listening to free-form jazz and 'writing what you feel'. Instead, creativity is about the same diligent and persistent hard work that brings success in every other subject and discipline. At its core is the concept of professionalism. As Steven Pressfield puts it in *Turning Pro*, 'to defeat the self-sabotaging habits of procrastination, self-doubt, susceptibility to distraction, perfectionism and shallowness, we enlist the self-strengthening habits of order, regularity, discipline and a constant striving after excellence'.[1]

ADDRESSING MISCONCEPTIONS

Establishing ground rules will be important, particularly if students have some partially formed sense of what creativity is. They will need clear messages about the culture, expectations and parameters when they're approaching a project in a new and unexpected way. Building a manifesto – a set of principles and ground rules – also requires us to spend some time surfacing and addressing some misconceptions about 'learning to be creative', all of which help to build a positive and purposeful working environment.

Here are ten principles we've found to be indispensable. We explore these ideas all the time, expressing them repeatedly in different ways. We've found that each one is good for busting a myth or misconception.

Principle 1: Writing successful narrative fiction is the result of a creative process that goes on for many weeks and months before the exam. This process can be taught, learned and engaged with over a long period of time.

Good for tackling: 'The exam is random. There's no reliable way to prepare. I'm going to go in there and wing it on the day, so these lessons are a waste of time.'

---

1   Steven Pressfield, *Turning Pro: Tap Your Inner Power and Create Your Life's Work* (New York: Black Irish Entertainment, 2010), p. 103.

Principle 2: Becoming a good writer of narrative fiction means being professional: not waiting for inspiration to strike but working hard to hunt it down.

Good for tackling: 'This will be easy. It'll be a chance to kick back, relax, mess about and wait for an idea to come.'

Principle 3: Good stories are the result of stockpiling a huge number of ideas and sorting through the ordinary to find the unusual or interesting. Ideas arrive in pieces (micro-ideas) and stories have to be built from these pieces. Original is overrated. All story components have been used somewhere before, but that doesn't stop you building something new with them.

Good for tackling: 'I don't have any ideas. I'll never get any. All my ideas are rubbish. They're not original.'

Principle 4: Good writers of narrative fiction read a lot of narrative fiction.

Good for tackling: 'I can write well without reading. I've watched a ton of movies. I'm the exception to the rule.'

Principle 5: There are a thousand different ways to tell a good story. Creativity is an act of courage – of beginning your version of a story without knowing if it will be successful or if other people will like it.

Good for tackling: 'How will I know when I'm "right"? I don't want to be "wrong" and look stupid.'

Principle 6: There's no such thing as writer's block.

Good for tackling: 'I'm blocked. I can't do anything today.'

Principle 7: Quantity beats quality. We arrive at good writing on the other side of bad writing. You can't edit a blank page.

Good for tackling: 'I admit I've only done a paragraph, but it's perfect. You're going to love it. Quality beats quantity.'

Principle 8: Very few stories turn out as the writer hoped. The story in our head is always better than the one we produce on the page. These failures are a normal part of the creative process.

Good for tackling: 'I'll have an idea for a story, I'll write it and the story will come out exactly as I'd hoped.'

Principle 9: Improvement comes from finding and making as many mistakes as possible, then learning from them. The more errors you make now, the fewer there are left to make in the exam.

Good for tackling: 'Once I get the hang of this it'll be easy. I'll get gradually better each time I write. Progress will be smooth and inevitable.'

Principle 10: Creativity is not a gift given to some and not others. We all have the capacity.

Good for tackling: 'You're born creative. It can't be taught. Sadly I'm not creative.'

We'll cover each of these in a little more detail in the following pages. As you'll no doubt be aware, attitude change is a long game – a slow and steady process of regular contact with new and unfamiliar ideas. Objections like the ones above will be repeated lesson after lesson. Our role is to quietly and patiently disagree, and offer stories, examples and research which continue to further an alternative version of the world.

A manifesto for a creative classroom gives us a new story to tell students about narrative writing.

PRINCIPLE 1:

WRITING SUCCESSFUL NARRATIVE FICTION IS THE RESULT OF A CREATIVE PROCESS THAT GOES ON FOR MANY WEEKS AND MONTHS BEFORE THE EXAM. THIS PROCESS CAN BE TAUGHT, LEARNED AND ENGAGED WITH OVER A LONG PERIOD OF TIME.

The creative production of any artefact — a short story, a poem or a song — is the end result of a period of preparation, thinking and planning (often subconscious) on the part of the creator. They may not know what the exam will ask, but confident students walk in with a healthy and well-fed imagination: a headful of ideas, starting points, characters, situations and possibilities. They've been engaged in a creative process in the weeks and months before the exam, often for longer. As a result, it's not unusual for these students to describe the exam experience as 'fun' or 'easy'.

THE CREATIVE PROCESS

Professor Giovanni Corazza, founder of the Marconi Institute of Creativity at the University of Bologna, speaks of the need 'to value long thinking' when exploring the creative process.[2] That is (in contrast to brilliant thinking, quick solutions or aha moments), thinking we stay with, that travels with us for a period of time and that takes us a long distance in a series of steps. Artist, entrepreneur and professor Raphael DiLuzio has a similar idea. He emphasises the importance of gestation, of holding an idea or problem in your head for a long period, often while doing other things.[3] This gestation, or long thinking, seems to be an important component in any creative endeavour.

It cannot, therefore, be done the night before the exam.

The best creative work done on the day of the creative writing paper will be the result of preparation, gestation and long thinking. There are many different ways of labelling the phases through which we pass during this long thinking. Here, we've synthesised a number of them. Our model is simple, clear and, we hope, easy to communicate.

---

2   Giovanni Corazza, 'Creative Thinking: How To Get Out of the Box and Generate Ideas' [video], *TEDxRoma* (11 March 2014). Available at: https://www.youtube.com/watch?v=bEusrD8g-dM.

3   Raphael DiLuzio, '7 Steps of Creative Thinking' [video], *TEDxDirigo* (28 June 2012). Available at: https://www.youtube.com/watch?v=MRD-4Tz60KE.

It's called FORGE, and it assumes that a problem or challenge has been set or generated – you can't create without one.

F – FEEDING

Our preparation (or long thinking if you prefer that term) needs fuel. Without this fuel, we operate with a weak imagination starved of stimuli. Our diet needs to be rich and varied and we must feed the imagination with a range of alternative inputs. As writer Haruki Murakami has commented, 'If you only read the books that everyone else is reading, you can only think what everyone else is thinking.'[4] The same goes for TV shows, narrative computer games and graphic novels.

Feeding gives the imagination a set of tropes, characters, situations, ideas and possibilities with which to experiment. It gives us more to imitate, emulate or steal (more about this in Principle 3). Of course, even with a lot to steal, we need to know how to adjust and adapt it so that it suits the vehicle of narrative prose.

A limited diet produces a number of issues:

- **The computer-game-only diet**: Students whose main inputs are computer games often try to reproduce the action of the game on the page, describing in a single sentence how a handily positioned bazooka allows their protagonist to clear the ground for a helicopter coming in to land. This scene, recently submitted in one of our sessions, patently didn't work on the page. The thrill of gaming is in the agency of the player-character and the immersion in a carefully built world. Turning it into prose without adjustment doesn't work.

- **The movies-only diet**: Here you may find the tendency to overwrite chase or action sequences so they become tedious blow-by-blow accounts devoid of drama, or to outline a long plot in an emotionless list of actions. They may have been good to watch but they're terrible to read.

- **The sport-only diet**: The reason there isn't a bestselling novel which gives us a real-time prose description of a tennis match is because prose often renders sporting drama inert. The dramatic power of a sporting occasion lies in its visceral immediacy. Therefore, if a sporting event is to be included in a story, we'd recommend that it is only as a backdrop to a more immediate and dramatic

---

4   Haruki Murakami [Tweet] (4 April 2013). Available at: https://twitter.com/harukimurakami_/status/319968161669730305?lang=en.

episode better suited to narrative prose. It's tempting to try to engage sports fans by encouraging a piece describing a contest or sporting occasion, but we've never yet read a powerful and engaging account of, say, a football match. Often, the pieces simply amount to hero worship. The same goes for students writing about live music or celebrity meetings, both of which rarely work well in fiction.

The books-from-childhood-only diet: There's nothing wrong with occasionally returning to favourite books, unless it is the sole fare. We needn't direct criticism at the Year 8 students still reading Wimpy Kid books, unless they're the only books being read. Kinney's books work tremendously well on a number of levels, but they're in diary form, obviously, so only showcase a first-person informal narrative. The same goes for other hugely popular diary-based writing: they are loosely structured and episodic, as a diary inevitably is, so they don't help to illustrate the plotting of short narratives. Kinney is first and foremost a cartoonist, so the humour works through the juxtaposition of prose and illustration – a technique the students won't be able to emulate later in the exam.

The graphic-novels-only diet: Graphic novels and interactive fiction are great at encouraging reading, as long as the young reader-writer can see beyond the self-imposed limitations of these genres as they gear up to write narrative prose. When we try to reproduce visual media in words, the results can be disappointing. In interactive fiction, characters other than the protagonist exist only to interact with the player-reader – they have no wishes or desires of their own. Readers need to be aware of this when they immerse themselves in interactive worlds.[5]

Feeding must include reading narrative prose. This process is so important that it gets a section of the manifesto to itself (see Principle 4). As to what should be read, the key is variety: short stories, middle grade (MG) or young adult (YA) novels, police procedurals and murder mysteries, thrillers, romances, family dramas, humorous diaries, superhero comics, graphic novels and childhood favourites.

It should go without saying, but for the sake of clarity, there are a vanishingly small number of circumstances in which we should be discouraging reading. If you're working with a member of staff or know of someone who is disparaging students' reading choices on the basis of quality, tackle them! We are not the gatekeepers or arbiters of taste.

---

5 For a superb exploration of many other things that don't work on the page – slapstick comedy, for example – see Howard Mittelmark and Sandra Newman's *How NOT to Write a Novel: 200 Mistakes to Avoid at All Costs if You Ever Want to Get Published* (London: Penguin, 2009), which contains some terrific takedowns of badly written narrative prose, many of which we've been guilty of ourselves.

O R – OBSERVING AND RESEARCHING

There is vigorous and healthy debate on the extent to which creativity requires knowledge. One on side, the argument goes that innovation can happen as a result of playful experimentation, using the knowledge we already have. On the other, the contention is that creativity is heightened by knowing lots – that it is a broad knowledge base that allows us to make creative connections and combinations.

Dr Tina Seelig of Stanford University emphasises that 'Your knowledge is the toolbox for your imagination.'[6] Seelig is firmly in the second camp. Our section on feeding aligns us with Seelig: the more you've read, the more tricks and tropes you've seen. The more you've seen and know, the better you can combine them creatively. Observation, research, speculation and discussion are all part of this phase.

Seelig asks us to 'pay attention' to the world around us. Our observation should be heightened and our knowledge deepened during this phase of the creative process. We read critically, we take notes during an online documentary, we walk the streets with fresh eyes, we people-watch, we google strange topics.

Martin was once teaching a session on landscape in literature in preparation for a coursework submission. It was a sunny day and he took his class outside and stood them by the school's reception area. The campus was on a rise above the town. In the distance were rolling hills of Pennine moorland. The students were asked to begin listing all the interesting elements of the landscape they could see below them – there was plenty to take in and comment on. They could have begun writing about:

- The rural vs. urban landscape/natural vs. built environment.

- The industrial landscape.

- Transport and travel – motorways, flyovers, roads and pathways.

- The religious landscape – church spires punctuating the view.

- Wildness.

- Population density – neighbourhoods, ghettos, integration and difference.

---

6 Tina Seelig, 'A Crash Course in Creativity' [video], *TEDxStanford* (1 August 2012). Available at: https://www.youtube.com/watch?v=gyM6rx69iqg. See also her excellent: *InGenius: A Crash Course on Creativity* (London: Hay House UK, 2012).

▢ The sky – weather and climate.

▢ Class, privilege, wealth and housing.

The next fifteen minutes were excruciating. Though some got a lot out of the session, many students had to repeatedly ask what they were meant to be looking at or looking for. Some had nothing to report by the end of the session. Others had a cursory note or two. Maybe the task was a bad one: seeing a familiar place in new ways can be challenging. We've since spent time discussing the process of observation. It requires practice. Good writing comes from observing the way the world is, the way people behave, the things they say to each other when waiting for a bus, the way environments change when it rains, the way headlights glitter in rush hour queues.

In the observing and researching phases we begin to gather these observations, thoughts, impressions and partially conceived possibilities. (We'll call these *micro-ideas* – more about them in Principle 3.) They arrive in small pieces and we make a note of them.

A note about notes: thousands of brilliant little micro-ideas are lost every day. They shoot temporarily through the mind ('Hey! What if ...?') and then they're gone. They die unrecorded. We'd suggest establishing a culture of collecting and capturing everything, no matter how insignificant, unimportant or uninspiring it may seem at the time. Issue each student with a jotter or exercise book or encourage the collection of ideas using the notes function on smartphones. Students should list ideas un-judgementally. Avoid checking them or looking them over yourself – these can be journals of possibilities.

Eventually the students will reach a point where the ideas they read over no longer look like their own – they've forgotten they even occurred to them. They become free story ideas: gifts from the past to the present self.

G E – GESTATION AND EXPERIMENTATION

We carry our emerging thoughts around with us and then begin combining them in new and unusual ways. Often we're detached – we go and do something else. We might, as Balder Onarheim, associate professor in creativity at the Technical University of Denmark, suggests, 'prime our sleep' by mentally examining the problem and our micro-ideas before we drop off.[7]

---

7   Balder Onarheim, '3 Tools to Become More Creative' [video], *TEDxCopenhagenSalon* (20 January 2015). Available at: https://www.youtube.com/watch?v=g-YScywp6AU.

Here are two examples of sleep priming that may be useful to share with your students:

1. Nobel Prize-winning chemist Linus Pauling gave a famous talk about creativity called 'The Genesis of Ideas' in which he explored sleep priming and long thinking. We love sharing the following: 'Sometimes I would think about the same problem for several nights in succession, while I was reading or making calculations about the problem during the day ... Some weeks or months might go by, and then, suddenly, an idea that represented a solution ... would burst into my consciousness.'[8] (We use Pauling when discussing creativity with students whose inclinations might be towards more scientific, logical thinking. His talk also includes the observation: 'A creative scientist is an artist – an artist whose ideas are in the field of science.')

2. From a different discipline, the novelist Stephen King, clearly a proponent of sleep priming, asserts the following in the introduction to his novel *The Green Mile*: 'I try to keep a story handy for those nights when sleep won't come. Each night I start over at the beginning ... writing them in my mind just as I would on a typewriter.'[9] Creating *The Green Mile* wasn't an easy process: 'The story wouldn't work for me. I tried it a hundred different ways ... and it still wouldn't work.' The solution, King tells us, didn't arrive until a year and a half later. Long thinking indeed.

What Pauling and King are reflecting on is a combination of gestation and experimentation. Each night King was reconfiguring his story and trying new micro-components. He was experimenting.

The long-thinking aspect of FORGE has been particularly useful in informing what we tell students about the creative process and when we start preparing them for the exam. This will be a long game – at least a two-year process. All elements of FORGE happen at the same time. We're feeding at the same time as we observe and research; we're gestating one idea as we experiment with another.

To return to the misconception at the start of this chapter, yes, the exam may be unpredictable. But there is a way to prepare, and anyone who prepares in this way will do much better than those who try to wing it on the day.

---

8   Linus Pauling, 'The Genesis of Ideas'. Speech delivered at the Third World Congress of Psychiatry, Montreal, 7 June 1961. Available at http://scarc.library.oregonstate.edu/coll/pauling/calendar/1961/06/7.html#1961s2.7.tei.xml.

9   Stephen King, *The Green Mile* (London: Gollancz, 2008), pp. 1–2.

For us, the forging process is continuous. We don't move around the cycle once – we're permanently forging something. We might be working on twenty or thirty micro-ideas, picking them up where we left them last time we were considering them, coming back to them, improving them and leaving them to gestate a little longer.

As we'll emphasise later, abundance is key!

FORGING – THEN CRAFTING

There comes a point in every creative endeavour when the forging process continues in the background but the crafting begins. We start to write experimentally to see what our idea looks like in prose.

Many students will be reluctant to get going, particularly those concerned with pre-serving perfection. Until we put pen to paper the story remains theoretical and its form perfect. The American painter Nathan Oliveira is often credited with the following observation: 'All art is a series of recoveries from the first line. The hardest thing to do is to put down the first line.' It's the same with narrative writing. All stories are a series of recoveries from the first line. The opening sentence won't be as good as we want it to be. We try to compensate with a good second sentence, which won't be quite what we were after either. We go again, composing a third line. All the time we're recovering. We've written entire novels that are recoveries – shadows of what we intended.

As teachers we can understand a student's reluctance, but we can't condone or allow it. Crafting is the only stage that ultimately matters – it continues to feed the whole process. Often, the early stages of writing are part of the experimentation phase because they immediately feed further thought. The inclusion of a particular character causes unforeseen problems and we experiment further, perhaps removing the character, changing the point of view or adjusting the location.

THE CRAFTING PROCESS

When switching our classes from forging to crafting, we need to provide clarity, expectation and management. Fearful crafters won't want to leave the relative safety of the planning process, and they will need safety and guidance. Here are seven ways you might make the process easier.

1. INTRODUCE FLOW

Martin wrote extensively about flow in *The GCSE Mindset*,[10] and that work is loosely reproduced here. Hungarian-American psychologist Mihaly Csikszentmihalyi first coined the term 'flow' in the 1960s, using it to describe a state of fully engaged, fluid and trance-like work. In an interview with John Geirland in 1996, Csikszentmihalyi describes a feeling of complete immersion in an activity, so that nothing else seems to matter: 'The ego falls away. Time flies … Your whole being is involved, and you're using your skills to the utmost.'[11]

Discuss experiences of flow with your class. The chances are that all students have felt it, perhaps while running or swimming, painting or playing music. It is active in nature; you're not in flow while passively watching a movie, but you may be when playing a

---

10 Steve Oakes and Martin Griffin, *The GCSE Mindset: Activities for Transforming Student Commitment, Motivation and Productivity* (Carmarthen: Crown House Publishing, 2017).

11 John Geirland, 'Go with the Flow' [interview with Mihaly Csikszentmihalyi], *Wired* (1 September 1996). Available at: https://www.wired.com/1996/09/czik/.

computer game. It's the purposeful absorption brought on by challenging and engaging work.

A vast number of interviews with dancers, musicians, rock climbers, artists, surgeons, chess players and, of course, writers convinced Csikszentmihalyi of the existence of flow states. Later in his career he turned his attention to the factors that contribute to the creation of these states. He suggested there were ten,[12] but the four that most interest us are:

1. Clear goals, expectations and rules: an awareness of what the aims are and what makes a good performance. (A student who recognises this might head into a period of writing thinking: 'I should be silent and focused. I should be building pictures in my mind, moving the story forward, then recording what I see. I'm moving away from the empty page towards paragraphs of prose.')

2. High levels of concentration and absorption – a 'limited' task free from the contradiction, chaos or confusion of everyday life. (Students aware of this often chunk the creative process: 'All I'm doing is describing this character getting out of a taxi and crossing the square on a rainy night. I just have to put down what happens next.')

3. A feeling of control – as if the self and the action are one and the same; decisions arise in constant spontaneous response to the task. (Students clear on this point might be thinking: 'It's just me, the paper and the words. Nothing else matters and no one is judging me.')

4. Immediate feedback, often from the self when reading over, checking and adjusting; a sense of whether things are going well or need further work. (Students aware of this are regularly rereading, editing and improving as they go along: 'I've not got the right word here. I need to cross this out and replace it. Maybe I need to add some dialogue here?')

Once students know what a flow state is, you can use the language to describe what classroom-based writing sessions should look and feel like, and then work continuously to create a culture in which flow can happen for short periods of time.

---

12 Mihaly Csikszentmihalyi, *Finding Flow: The Psychology of Discovery and Invention* (New York: Harper Perennial, 1997).

2. TIME-LIMITED SESSIONS

Since flow takes a little time to reach, super-short sessions haven't been helpful for us. When we ran sessions with six-minute writing exercises, some were happy to run down the clock and do nothing. Others needed longer. Somewhere between eight and twelve minutes has worked well: long enough for silence to establish itself and for the students to realise you mean it, but short enough so that those who are experiencing difficulties aren't trapped clockwatching forever. As levels of concentration and discipline increase, so can the length of the sessions.

3. HANDWRITING BEATS TYPING

It might just be us, but whenever our students sit at individual laptops or PCs, they type a sentence and then spend fifteen minutes seeing what it looks like in every available font.

4. MODELLING

Some of our best sessions have occurred when we are writing too. This has multiple advantages:

- You're at the front showing students how it's done.

- You're not patrolling. Flow is hard to reach if your primary concern is hiding your work whenever your teacher hovers at your shoulder.

- You're not tempted to sit with one student working through a problem while levels of concentration drop all around you. And before you know it you're reduced to bellowing, 'We should be working IN SILENCE!' from a seated position somewhere among the kids.

- You're not robbing the students of their feelings of control by judging them as they go.

- You can read your work aloud to encourage others to share theirs too. (It goes without saying that your role here is to lower your status by sharing flawed work, not to blow them away with heart-rending purple prose!)

5. MUSIC

Don't roll your eyes! This has worked particularly well for us when the music is chosen to suit the session. It's always film scores, usually orchestral and always without lyrics. We've experimented with film scores in lots of different situations and the result is often a heightening of concentration. The music must be unobtrusive and atmospheric. There is no negotiation on the topic of music; no concessions given. You aren't going to take requests, so put away *High School Musical*.

Instead consider the following – all available on Spotify:

- Jeff Beal's *House of Cards* score or his work for *Gypsy*.
- Alexandre Desplat's music for *The Danish Girl*, *The Ides of March*, *The Painted Veil* or *Syriana*.
- Anne Dudley's score for *Elle* or her music for *Poldark*.
- Harry Gregson-Williams' scores for *The Zookeeper's Wife*, *The Equalizer 2*, *Déjà Vu* or *Breath*.
- James Newton Howard's work for *Snow Falling on Cedars*, *The Lady in the Water*, *Concussion* or *Michael Clayton*.
- Thomas Newman's work for *He Named Me Malala*, *The Shawshank Redemption*, *The Green Mile*, *The Debt* or *Revolutionary Road*.
- Rachel Portman's score for *Never Let Me Go* or *Despite the Falling Snow*.
- Hans Zimmer's music for *The Thin Red Line* or *Frost/Nixon*.

Note: there will be naysayers – usually staff rather than students.

6. NON-SUBMISSION

Not all written pieces need marking. Often announcing at the start of a session that the work won't be shared or marked yet, that it's too early in the crafting process to be making assessments, helps to free up writers and encourages experimentation and risk-taking.

7. WHAT'S YOUR FAVOURITE BIT?

It's important to acknowledge that none of us will be completely happy with what we've produced, but there will be something – a word, a phrase, an image, a line of dialogue – that we're probably pleased with. Students get to reread and adjust their work, then highlight or underline something they're happy to have produced. You could do the same. These gems are reusable. It's fine if they appear again in the next attempt.

PRINCIPLE 2:

BECOMING A GOOD WRITER OF NARRATIVE FICTION MEANS BEING PROFESSIONAL: NOT WAITING FOR INSPIRATION TO STRIKE BUT WORKING HARD TO HUNT IT DOWN.

Creativity isn't cushy or easy. Steven Pressfield, in his book *The War of Art*, identifies the belief in waiting for creativity to happen as one manifestation of what he calls resistance – the force that is forever trying to stop us from creating art. To overcome this requires great self-discipline and control, but it also requires professionalism.[13] This, in part, is the act of turning up to do the job and doing it diligently.

A common stereotype of the writer is of a tortured soul whose inspiration has been blocked. The inspiration is some spiritual muse, a supernatural force that swoops down and touches the forehead of the writer, filling them with brilliant art.

It's a load of nonsense.

Most authors are small businesses. They rely on writing to pay their bills and feed their families. They don't have time to sit around waiting for inspiration to strike. Most of the authors we know are out there hunting for writing jobs and actively searching for commercial ideas that they can sell to publishing houses, media companies and agents.

So, forget the muses. We need to be a classroom of professionals.

Professionals turn up to do the job of writing and ignore any negative voices. Professionals know that all writing has a purpose. Students should be aware of that purpose, whether it's impressing the teacher or an examiner. We often assume an audience for the purposes of our writing – a leaflet for newly arrived students or a letter of complaint to a newspaper – but, in reality, the purpose of any writing is to demonstrate that we have the skills to write in that form. Inviting the students to be professional about their work enables them to see its true purpose.

The professional mindset is expressed with brutal clarity by Steven Pressfield in his book *Turning Pro*: 'The professional acts in the face of fear. The professional is prepared. The professional does not hesitate to ask for help. The professional is committed over

---

13 Steven Pressfield, *The War of Art: Break Through the Blocks and Win Your Inner Creative Battles* (New York: Black Irish Entertainment, 2002).

the long haul. The professional dedicates himself to mastering technique. The professional reinvents herself.'[14]

Professionals get to grips with the rules of their craft. In *Psychology Today*, Jeffrey Loewenstein and Matthew Cronin, authors of *The Craft of Creativity*, talk about creativity using the example of a gourmet meal.[15] You need the skills and the ingredients to be creative with food. The ability to create a gourmet meal comes with learning the craft: the right temperature to cook at, when to take a sauce off the boil, how to chop and dice quickly, and which flavours go together so you can challenge that assumption. Writing is no different: you need to master the craft and know the ingredients of a genre before you can write and subvert them.

---

14 Pressfield, *Turning Pro*, pp. 90–91.

15 Jeffrey Loewenstein and Matthew Cronin, 'Creativity: Think Gourmet Meals, Not Magic Moments', *Psychology Today* (9 May 2018). Available at: https://www.psychologytoday.com/gb/blog/the-craft-creativity/201805/creativity-think-gourmet-meals-not-magic-moments.

PRINCIPLE 3:

GOOD STORIES ARE THE RESULT OF STOCKPILING A HUGE NUMBER OF IDEAS AND SORTING THROUGH THE ORDINARY TO FIND THE UNUSUAL OR INTERESTING. IDEAS ARRIVE IN PIECES (MICRO-IDEAS) AND STORIES HAVE TO BE BUILT FROM THESE PIECES. ORIGINAL IS OVERRATED. ALL STORY COMPONENTS HAVE BEEN USED SOMEWHERE BEFORE, BUT THAT DOESN'T STOP YOU BUILDING SOMETHING NEW WITH THEM.

Often there's a misconception about what an idea is. Students who claim they don't have any ideas, or any *good ideas*, usually mean 'I don't have a fully formed idea,' 'I don't have a complete idea,' 'I don't have a startlingly original idea' or 'I don't have an idea I really love.' You don't need any of these things. You need a collection of micro-ideas.

MICRO-IDEAS

What do we class as an idea? The British Library's archive audio collection *The Writing Life* has fascinating interviews with countless authors.[16] Hilary Mantel's description of what an idea is struck us as helpful. She likens an idea to a granule of grit. It's small and seemingly insignificant, but if it has promise, things accrete around it and it grows. Whether into a pearl or not remains to be seen.

As the name suggests, micro-ideas are small — expressed as a sentence, a phrase or perhaps just a word. They're rough and unformed. Often they're lifeless until they're combined with another idea. Stronger ideas come, says Will Gompertz in *Think Like an Artist*, 'when we encourage our brain to combine at least two apparently random elements in a new way'.[17] Take Suzanne Collins' story of how she conceived of The Hunger Games trilogy: 'One night, I was lying in bed, and I was channel surfing between reality TV programs and actual war coverage,' she tells the *School Library Journal*. 'On one channel, there's a group of young people competing for I don't even know; and on the next, there's a group of young people fighting in an actual war. That's the moment when Katniss's story came to me.'[18]

---

16 British Library, *The Writing Life: Authors Speak* [audiobook] (London: British Library Sound Archive, 2011).

17 Will Gompertz, *Think Like an Artist ... and Lead a More Creative, Productive Life* (London: Penguin, 2015), p. 80.

18 Rick Margolis, 'A Killer Story: An Interview with Suzanne Collins, Author of *The Hunger Games*', *School Library Journal* (1 September 2008). Available at: https://www.slj.com/?detailStory=a-killer-story-an-interview-with-suzanne-collins-author-of-the-hunger-games.

Not everyone will see the potential of micro-ideas when considered alone. Students might raise a world-weary eyebrow at a number of them. But as Hilary Mantel testifies, ideas tend to have magnetism. They gather an accretion of other ideas. Some micro-ideas gather stronger magnetism and attract more thoughts and ideas.

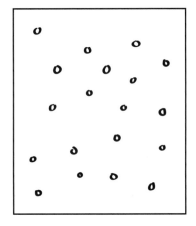

Micro-ideas

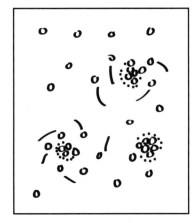

Connected ideas
become magnetic!

The 'good idea' that a student is mistakenly assuming should arrive in one piece might be an accumulation of four or five micro-ideas. As Picasso famously said, 'I begin with an idea, and then it becomes something else.'[19]

You might consider sharing micro-ideas and asking students to experimentally combine them. Here's an example we used with some Year 8 students recently. We shared a bank of micro-ideas we had previously recorded ourselves (don't judge: like all micro-ideas they may strike you as insignificant, inert or dull) and asked students to combine them. The micro-ideas they decided to use were:

▪ A stately home in a rainstorm.

▪ Two sisters – one happy, one sad (Why?).

▪ Wild creatures from another planet (like dinosaurs?).

19 Quoted in Gompertz, *Think Like an Artist*, p. 82.

- A boy with an eyepatch.
- Being trapped overnight (hotel?) with the ghost of the guy who last slept there.

The story summary that emerged was as follows:

> A wild jungle planet is used as a hunting base for rich people from Earth. There's a big fancy mansion surrounded by a high fence. There, a group of adults and their children gather. The monsters break free and terrorise them, killing them one by one. There's also a ghost who only the sisters can see and talk to – a boy with an eyepatch.

Many were enthusiastically plotting and planning by the end of the session. Plenty were excited: they felt they had got something fresh and interesting by carefully choosing, discarding and combining micro-ideas. Bearing this in mind, you might want to make the early stages of creative work about creating a visually accessible bank of fifty or a hundred micro-ideas. Go for more if you can. They could include:

- Character names.
- Possible locations.
- A single scene.
- A strange opening.
- A phrase, word or saying.
- A character trait.
- A weird situation.

Letting students withdraw because they have one good idea is dangerous and not to be recommended. Abundance is key!

Roger von Oech, president of Creative Think, game designer and creativity expert, puts it this way: 'If you only have one idea, you only have one course of action open to you ... risky in a world where flexibility is a requirement for survival.'[20] The exam is a world where flexibility is a requirement for survival – a point that needs constant emphasis.

---

20 Roger von Oech, *A Whack on the Side of the Head: How You Can Be More Creative* (Menlo Park, CA: Creative Think, 1983), p. 26.

Tom and David Kelley explore the notion of abundance in *Creative Confidence*. 'When ideas are in short supply, it's tempting to become possessive and limit your options,' they point out. 'If you have only a few ideas in your idea bank, you're more likely to settle on one of the few you have and defend it fiercely ... but when ideas are plentiful and easy ... there's no need to become territorial about them.'[21]

Keep encouraging collection until you have your fifty or a hundred or more. Get the students to record them all. Take the ideas jotters in at the end of sessions and keep them safe. Assure the students that you won't be checking them.

CONSTRAINT FUELS CREATIVITY

In 2015, Aadil Vora (a medical student at the time) delivered a fascinating TEDx talk about creativity.[22] In it he outlined his experiences of coaching elementary school students in a creativity competition called 'Odyssey of the Mind'. One activity gives students the plain image of a clock face with a red second hand. The instruction is: *Replace the second hand with something unique.* The aim is to make the clock more interesting and unusual. Have a go!

Now let's examine some of the responses Vora got from his students. We've labelled them A–J and arranged them in reverse alphabetical order. It might be interesting to give each response a quick score. Use the 1–5 scale on the left.

5 Most Creative	A	Witch's Finger
	B	Twig
4	C	Toothpick
	D	Stick Insect
3 Good	E	Spoon
	F	Oar
	G	Needle
2	H	Giraffe
	I	Dinosaur's Tail
1 Common	J	Angelina Jolie's Right Leg

---

21 Tom Kelley and David Kelley, *Creative Confidence: Unleashing the Creative Potential within Us All* (New York: Crown Business, 2014), p. 82.

22 Aadil Vora, 'Trick Your Mind into Being Creative' [video], *TEDxNSU* (7 May 2015). Available at: https://www.youtube.com/watch?v=1xWa3Ok2e94.

Now you've scribbled down some thoughts, here's the interesting part. Not all these responses were generated under the same conditions.

▪ Some students were given free rein: *Replace the second hand with something unique.*

▪ Some were given a specific constraint: *Replace the second hand with something unique. It has to be green.*

▪ And some were given a different constraint: *Replace the second hand with something unique. It has to be alive.*

Here are the responses organised by limitation:

	Responses	Your scores
Free rein	Twig, toothpick, spoon, oar, needle	
Something green	Witch's finger, dinosaur's tail	
Something alive	Stick insect, giraffe, Angelina Jolie's right leg	

If your scores are anything like ours, or the hundreds of students who've since taken part in this scoring experiment with us, the responses generated with constraints get a higher score than those generated in complete freedom. (The 'free' responses, incidentally, tend towards physical stand-ins or similarly shaped objects.)

Consider sharing this with your students (we like doing this!) and then give them some constraints to use. By insisting on a focus you are providing a structure or framework to their writing. Professional writers do this to themselves all the time. Here are five constraints you might want to consider:

1. Insist that the writers place themselves in the story. They are the narrators. This can have the effect of situating their story in the real world, even if strange and fantastic things happen.

2. Dictate the setting: a shopping centre, a fairground, a busy office. Again, this can guide writers as to the types of characters they might meet. A picture stimulus is appropriate for this exercise.

3. Give them a story trope or genre to invert or subvert. Inversion might be a reverse heist story in which the thieves have to return something without being caught. Subversion might be a hero from classical mythology who turns out to be a total coward.

4. List three objects or people that must appear in the story: a torch, a bucket and a mop; a shop assistant, an old woman and a store detective. Obviously, the object may dictate the genre of story: a coffin, a crucifix and a wooden stake will easily lead to a tale of vampires. What if you subvert that list? Challenge students to write a story with a coffin, a crucifix and a wooden stake that *doesn't* have any vampires in it.

5. Dictate an everyday activity and then place it in an unusual setting: going shopping in a warzone, or a family outing in the jungle.

Your first idea is rarely your best (we'll explore this in Activity 1). Many of our early ideas fall short of what we consider to be original or interesting. They're often clichéd. 'Discount the 1st thing that comes to mind,' advises Pixar storyboard artist Emma Coats. 'And the 2nd, 3rd, 4th, 5th – get the obvious out of the way. Surprise yourself.'[23]

DISNEY'S THREE ROOMS

You may be familiar with the details of Disney's creative approach but the chances are that your students won't. It's well worth sharing. According to Michael Michalko, author of *Cracking Creativity* and *Thinkertoys*, the master storyteller required his concept artists, storyboarders and animators to function with three distinct roles:

1. **The dreamer**: 'A dreamer spins innumerable fantasies, wishes, outrageous hunches and bold and absurd ideas without limit or judgment.'

2. **The realist**: 'The realist [turns] the dreamer's ideas into something realistic and feasible.'

---

23 See Cyriaque Lamar, 'The 22 Rules of Storytelling, According to Pixar', *io9* (8 June 2012). Available at: https://io9.gizmodo.com/5916970/the-22-rules-of-storytelling-according-to-pixar.

3. **The critic**: 'The critic reviews all the ideas and tries to punch holes in them.'[24]

Disney physically moved his staff from room to room to indicate a shift in role and to keep them focused. Room 1 was the room to dream in, room 2 was where the realists took over and room 3 was the place to be critical.

Students who dismiss their own ideas as 'rubbish' move too swiftly from dreamer to critic, which hamstrings them before they've had a chance to establish themselves – or gather a few other ideas around them. Students who are too loyal to ideas that aren't working might lack the no-nonsense approach of the critic. 'Every creative person needs a room three,' argues Scott Belsky in *Making Ideas Happen*. 'The idea bloodshed that occurs in room three is just as important as the wild ideation of room one.'[25]

Sharing Disney's technique with your students – and insisting they stay in each role for a longer period – will help to create a climate in which students can non-judgementally generate a stack of micro-ideas.

THE IMPORTANCE OF IMITATION AND THEFT

Look at the early work of any artist and you will see an impersonator yet to find his or her own voice.

Will Gompertz, *Think Like an Artist*

We all start off by copying. Martin wrote Doctor Who fan fiction and once impressed his creative writing tutor by submitting poetry composed entirely of stolen song lyrics. Jon wrote numerous fantasy stories: carbon copies of *Lord of the Rings* and *Conan* that involved wizards and elves, barbarians and orcs. He also used to write and draw his own versions of Marvel Comics. A pre-designed universe populated by fully realised characters means nascent writers can shortcut their way to practice, just like the aspiring piano player who hammers out stilted covers one slow note at a time. Students need to dismiss the judgemental inner critic who tells them, 'This is no good. It's been

---

24 Michael Michalko, 'Walt Disney's Creative Thinking Technique', *Creative Thinking* (29 August 2011). Available at: http://creativethinking.net/walt-disney%E2%80%99s-creative-thinking-technique/#sthash.EZ4qZMpV.dpbs.

25 Scott Belsky, *Making Ideas Happen: Overcoming the Obstacles between Vision and Reality* (London: Penguin, 2010), p. 76.

done before.' After all, as Will Gompertz observes, 'you have to imitate before you can emulate'.[26]

This is an important point for any creative manifesto. Paying homage via imitation is all part of the process. Imitation becomes emulation becomes theft.

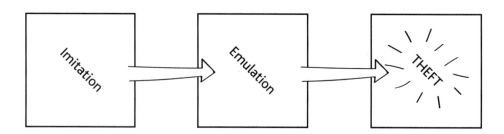

A word about the differences here:

Imitation is copying – producing a close facsimile of an admired source work without yet fully understanding it. (Perhaps *in order* to understand it?)

Emulation is producing a work that pays homage to a source, reproducing many parts of it but adding original elements, perhaps through subversion, inversion or parody. The writer is beginning to recognise how the source text works and can experiment within the constraints of its world. Fan fiction lives here.

Theft is sophisticated. It involves seeing the working parts of the source, recognising and assessing these subcomponents, stealing one or two, and recasting them in new and interesting ways. As screenwriter Paul Schrader (*Taxi Driver*) tells film-maker Brian Koppelman, 'You have to steal around. You can't go back to the same 7-Eleven. They catch you. [So] you go to the floral shop. Then you go to the gas station. Then the hot dog stand nobody goes to. And eventually somebody will think you made it up.'[27]

Artist Austin Kleon distinguishes the characteristics of good theft and bad theft in *Steal Like an Artist*. For example, he says that good theft honours rather than degrades.

---

26 Gompertz, *Think Like an Artist*, p. 86.

27 Brian Koppelman, 'The Moment with Brian Koppelman' [interview with Paul Schrader] [podcast], *Stitcher* (22 May 2018). Available at: https://www.stitcher.com/podcast/slate/the-moment-with-brian-koppelman/e/54581735.

According to Kleon, good theft transforms rather than merely imitates. It remixes rather than rips off. And, like Schrader, Kleon emphasises the need for rich and varied sources: 'There's an economic theory out there that if you take the incomes of your five closest friends and average them, the resulting number will be pretty close to your own income. I think the same is true of our idea incomes. You are only going to be as good as the stuff you surround yourself with.'[28]

The message for the student who feels they have to be original? There's nothing new under the sun. We're all working with the same material. Copying is a natural starting point, but the ultimate aim is to surround yourself with great work – then to steal around. To try to combine familiar elements in new and interesting ways.

---

28 Austin Kleon, *Steal Like an Artist* (New York: Workman, 2012), p. 13.

PRINCIPLE 4:

GOOD WRITERS OF NARRATIVE FICTION READ A LOT OF NARRATIVE FICTION.

Any writer worth their salt will tell you that reading and writing go hand in hand. Neither of us can name a writer who doesn't read for pleasure. Nor can we think of a writer who doesn't, at some level, read for research purposes.

In 2015, the Reading Agency commissioned a literature review of research related to reading for pleasure. From this, it drew some observations. Reading has a number of 'payoffs' for all sectors of society. For children, it encouraged empathy, improved attainment (even in maths and numeracy), helped with relaxation, focus and flow, and was essential in creative pursuits.

> The main outcomes reported were enjoyment, knowledge of the self and other people, social interaction, social and cultural capital, imagination, focus and flow, relaxation and mood regulation. Improvements in young children's communication abilities and longer-term education outcomes were also reported for early years children.[29]

The findings suggested that reading for pleasure could have a positive impact on children's attainment, but principally when they had a degree of control over their reading rather than for some external motivation. In their paper *Research Evidence on Reading for Pleasure*, the Education Standards Research Team highlighted the benefits for comprehension, general knowledge and reading attainment.[30] Reading gives access to new ideas, other cultures and unusual experiences. It gives students phrases, images, tropes and micro-ideas to play with and widens their vocabulary.

When we encounter a talented writer in school, they are nearly always a keen reader too. These readers are 'genre savvy': they know the tropes and character stereotypes of every book they have read. They will compare plotlines and characters between books and films. They will avoid what is clichéd and emulate what they admire. Confident and

---

29 Reading Agency, *Literature Review: The Impact of Reading for Pleasure and Empowerment* (June 2015). Available at: https://readingagency.org.uk/news/The%20Impact%20of%20Reading%20for%20 Pleasure%20and%20Empowerment.pdf, p. 4.

30 Department for Education, *Research Evidence on Reading for Pleasure: Education Standards Research Team* (May 2012). Available at: https://assets.publishing.service.gov.uk/government/uploads/system/uploads/ attachment_data/file/284286/reading_for_pleasure.pdf.

enthusiastic readers will often be braver in their experimentation with writing styles and borrow phrases from their favourite authors.

There are many ways to encourage reading for pleasure in schools: book boxes, a school library with an experienced and enthusiastic librarian, competitions, teachers as readers. This is not the remit of this book, however. Suffice to say that if you want to nurture and feed creativity in your classroom, make time for reading for pleasure and talking about books.

PRINCIPLE 5:

THERE ARE A THOUSAND DIFFERENT WAYS TO TELL A GOOD STORY. CREATIVITY IS AN ACT OF COURAGE – OF BEGINNING YOUR VERSION OF A STORY WITHOUT KNOWING IF IT WILL BE SUCCESSFUL OR IF OTHER PEOPLE WILL LIKE IT.

There is no right or wrong during the idea development phase. In the dreaming room, there's no such thing as a mistake.

In the past, we've both dismissed the notion of leaving a regular teaching job with pensions benefits and a regular salary to become writers as a stupid idea. Other people did that sort of thing. Not us. Similarly, we both encountered students who wouldn't commit to writing because their ideas might be thought of as stupid. Even worse were the students who destroyed their work before anyone could read it because they thought the same.

Jon was lucky enough to hear David Almond give a keynote speech entitled 'Daring to be Stupid' at the Federation of Children's Book Groups Conference in 2011. Almond confessed that every time he started a book, he was plagued with self-doubt and thought that everything he wrote was ridiculous. He invited the audience to see writing as an act of bravery. The writer was overcoming these negative feelings – daring to be stupid, if you will.

Many students don't like to appear too creative because they fear the judgement of their peers. But what is needed in class is the freedom to express ideas, an environment in which students can take creative risks more fearlessly.

Often, on hearing the word 'stupid', students assume you mean 'wacky' or 'bizarre'. Having discussed daring to be stupid at the start of a workshop, the students come up with ideas like unicorns driving clown cars and worlds made of sweets inhabited by talking cupcakes. While these might seem fun topics to write about, they rarely give the students the best chance to showcase their skills or to extend their story. They become trapped in a narrative of increasingly surreal events that leaves the reader bewildered and unamused. There has to be some discipline to the work, some focus to it.

A discussion about creative courage can set the foundations for a classroom safe enough for the wildest of ideas. We've found that students recognise the description of times when writing has been destroyed or chances missed because of the fear of peer judgement. It is worth discussing the pitfalls of trying to be open and suggest ideas in class. Talk about the idea of 'being stupid' and taking risks. Jon likes getting students to discuss their favourite online content, memes, YouTube clips and gifs. Which ones survive and go viral? Are they always the most sensible, or even the ones that you would have thought of first?

PRINCIPLE 6:

THERE'S NO SUCH THING AS WRITER'S BLOCK.

Plumbers don't get plumber's block and teachers don't get teacher's block. Writers shouldn't be allowed the luxury of pretending they're blocked, particularly since writer's block doesn't exist. The whole metaphor of writing as piped liquid (i.e. 'It's really flowing today!' or 'It seems to have dried up – I'm blocked') is to be avoided. Instead of water, try ice. In the preface to her autobiographical collection of essays *Yes Please*, American sitcom writer and comedian Amy Poehler asserts that 'writing this book has been like … hacking away at a freezer with a screwdriver'.[31] Poehler's image emphasises hard work over ease – chipping away with dogged persistence.

Seth Godin has written over twenty books. He also blogs every single day of the year and has done so for years. If anyone is likely to feel blocked, it's someone who has set themselves the challenge of blogging so regularly. And yet, for Godin, writer's block doesn't exist. 'Yes, we feel stuck,' Godin admits. But he goes on to argue that the feeling is fear. 'What we're really saying is, "I don't have any ideas that are perfectly formed. I don't have something that I'm sure is going to work."' A proponent of the quantity-beats-quality paradigm discussed on page 37, Godin concludes: 'Your problem isn't that you don't have enough good ideas. Your problem might be that you don't have enough bad ideas.'[32]

Bad writing, Godin argues, is what we do on the way to good writing.

---

31 Amy Poehler, *Yes Please* (London: Picador, 2015), p. 10.

32 Seth Godin, 'No Such Thing (As Writer's Block)' [podcast], *Art19* (2018). Available at: https://art19.com/shows/akimbo/episodes/6e6e4997-65e6-4b77-880f-124da99f05ba.

PRINCIPLE 7:

QUANTITY BEATS QUALITY. WE ARRIVE AT GOOD WRITING ON THE OTHER SIDE OF BAD WRITING. YOU CAN'T EDIT A BLANK PAGE.

Quality is the result of abundance, not the careful nurturing of a single idea or the desire to perfect a short piece. We're after rough, ready and plentiful. As Voltaire observes, 'Perfect is the enemy of good.'

Don't allow the 'quality narrative' to develop in class. For help, refer to David Bayles and Ted Orland's excellent *Art and Fear*. In it they tell a story about a ceramics teacher at an art school. (The story is probably apocryphal: short, powerful, truthful, much like a fable.) The teacher splits the ceramics students into two groups. On the left-hand side of the studio the students are encouraged to produce as much work as possible. Pot after pot – quantity is the aim. The work would simply be weighed at the end of the production period and grades assigned based on the amount of work produced. On the right-hand side of the class quality was the aim: 'Those being graded on "quality" ... needed to produce only one pot – albeit a perfect one – to get an "A".'

When grading the work, the teacher adjusted tack and decided to mark everything based on quality. A 'curious fact emerged', write Bayles and Orland, 'the works of highest quality were all produced by the group being graded for quantity'. The authors conclude: 'If you think good work is somehow synonymous with perfect work, you are headed for big trouble.'[33]

---

33 David Bayles and Ted Orland, *Art and Fear: Observations on the Perils (and Rewards) of Artmaking* (New York: Image Continuum, 1993), p. 29.

PRINCIPLE 8:

VERY FEW STORIES TURN OUT AS THE WRITER HOPED. THE STORY IN OUR HEAD IS ALWAYS BETTER THAN THE ONE WE PRODUCE ON THE PAGE. THESE FAILURES ARE A NORMAL PART OF THE CREATIVE PROCESS.

A good starting point for discussing failure in the context of a creative endeavour is Will Gompertz' excellent *Think Like an Artist*. At the heart of his argument is the notion that since none of us produce stories as good as the ones we imagine in our heads, all of us ultimately fail as writers. 'Which, if you think about it,' he says, 'makes the concept of failure close to meaningless.'[34]

The upfront knowledge that our efforts are doomed will not inspire dedicated practice, and it's not what Gompertz argues. Instead, he concludes that the writer knows that 'not everything we attempt works out as we had hoped. A far more important lesson to learn from artists is not that they fail, but that they prevail.'[35]

It's also well worth emphasising the *when* of failure, and the importance of amassing and processing a large number of errors before the exam, rather than on the day. 'The best kinds of failures,' note Tom and David Kelley, 'are quick, cheap and early, leaving you plenty of time to ... iterate your ideas.'[36]

Software engineer and project management guru Steve McConnell refers to 'thrashing' early.[37] That is, doing the difficult creative decision-making upfront: 'you explore all of the ideas for a project at the beginning, when it's most cost-effective'.[38] Thrashing is arguing, debating, questioning, failing, disassembling, ditching and reconceiving. In essence – fail early, and your project is likely to emerge the better for it. Students need to know that the early stages of a project can be messy. Messiness near the start may well be a very good thing.

Otherwise you end up in *Rogue One* territory.

---

34 Gompertz, *Think Like an Artist*, p. 42.

35 Gompertz, *Think Like an Artist*, p. 57.

36 Kelley and Kelley, *Creative Confidence*, p. 130.

37 Steve McConnell, 'The Power of Process' (1998). Available at: https://stevemcconnell.com/articles/the-power-of-process/.

38 See https://designbycosmic.com/insights/articles/thrash-and-sprint.

Screenwriter Tony Gilroy was paid a reported US$5 million to fix the *Star Wars* movie months before it was due to be released. It was allegedly confused, difficult to follow and varied wildly in tempo and tone. Speaking about the experience to the *Hollywood Reporter*, Gilroy said of the project: 'they were in terrible trouble'. Gilroy needed to do a complete overhaul – to find the heart of the story in order to fix it. 'If you look at *Rogue*, all the difficulty ... all the confusion ... in the end when you get in there, it's actually very, very simple to solve,' he says. 'Because you sort of go, "This is a movie where ... everyone is going to die." So it's a movie about sacrifice.'[39]

Still, 5 million US dollars – that's the high cost of thrashing at the end, not the beginning.

---

39 Aaron Couch, 'Tony Gilroy on "Rogue One" Reshoots: They Were in "Terrible Trouble", *Hollywood Reporter* (5 April 2018). Available at: https://www.hollywoodreporter.com/heat-vision/star-wars-rogue-one-writer-tony-gilroy-opens-up-reshoots-1100060.

PRINCIPLE 9:

IMPROVEMENT COMES FROM FINDING AND MAKING AS MANY MISTAKES AS POSSIBLE, THEN LEARNING FROM THEM. THE MORE ERRORS YOU MAKE NOW, THE FEWER THERE ARE LEFT TO MAKE IN THE EXAM.

Inconsistent execution is typical of the early stages of skill acquisition, and as such all writers should expect it. And since we don't follow a neat upward line of measurably improving writing as we go, there is a significant psychological element to continued application.

In *The Dip*, Seth Godin discusses the shape of a long-term project such as learning to play the piano, speak Italian, surf, ski, skateboard or to complete that novel you've always wanted to write. Why do so few of us become proficient pianists? Godin introduces the idea of the dip. 'At the beginning, when you first start something, it's fun. Over the next few days and weeks the rapid learning you experience keeps going,' he says. Then comes the dip. 'The Dip,' Godin explains, 'is the long slog between starting and mastery.'[40] If there was no dip, everyone would be a brilliant musician, a world-class skier or a surfing guru. The reason they aren't is that most of them quit when results stop improving. This is the dip – the place where progress temporarily flatlines. Beyond the dip is further forward movement, even though it might not feel that way.

Author and entrepreneur Scott Belsky's concept of the project plateau is similar. 'The project plateau is littered with the carcases of dead ideas that have never happened,' he says. 'What do we do? We just generate a new idea.' According to Belsky, when we reach a plateau our tendency is to ditch the hard project and start something new, so we can return to that excited feeling of beginning something. 'And this is why', he explains, 'there are more half-written novels in the world than there are novels.'[41]

Your students will hit the dip, but so will you. A certain number of sessions in and you'll feel hopeless: this isn't working, they still don't believe me. The dip is why teaching is rife with 'we tried that and it didn't work' narratives.

Here's what we've discovered. Being aware of the dip or the project plateau helps. Knowing it's there and expecting it makes the creative process easier (usually it comes

---

40 Seth Godin, *The Dip: The Extraordinary Benefits of Knowing When to Quit (and When to Stick)* (London: Piatkus, 2007), p. 17.

41 See Maria Popova, 'Scott Belsky on How to Avoid Idea Plateaus', *Brainpickings* (18 March 2011). Available at: https://www.brainpickings.org/2011/03/18/scott-belsky-idea-plateaus/.

at about 30,000 words on a 65,000 word project). It's a normal part of the process and should be included in your manifesto.

PRINCIPLE 10:

CREATIVITY IS NOT A GIFT GIVEN TO SOME AND NOT OTHERS. WE ALL HAVE THE CAPACITY.

David Bayles and Ted Orland make this interesting point in *Art and Fear*: 'Were talent a prerequisite, then the better the artwork, the easier it would have been to make.'[42] Was it easy for Leonardo da Vinci to paint the *Mona Lisa*? Was it easy for Quentin Tarantino to write and direct *Reservoir Dogs* or *The Hateful Eight*? Was it easy for J. K. Rowling to write the Harry Potter series? 'By definition,' conclude Bayles and Orland, 'whatever you have is exactly what you need to produce your best work. There is probably no clearer waste of psychic energy than worrying about ... talent.'[43]

Dr Kyung Hee Kim is a researcher in the field of creativity and the author of *The Creativity Challenge: How We Can Recapture American Innovation*, in which she dissects her own meta-analysis of creativity and age. As part of Kim's work, students at various ages/grades are asked to complete a creativity test and are scored for particular creative aptitudes. (We've included equivalent year groups for students in England in the quotes that follow.)

First the test: the Torrance Tests of Creative Thinking (TTCT) were developed by Ellis Paul Torrance and are a test of divergent thinking. It's worth pointing out that divergent thinking is only part of the creative process – the FORGE-ing part. It's important that we don't substitute 'divergent thinking' or 'idea generation' for 'creativity', since creativity, in the context of *Storycraft*, actually means creating: crafting, persisting through challenges, finishing a project and making something.

On to Kim's study. She divides creativity into various components and her findings are considerably more nuanced: 'Children's ability to produce ideas increased up to third grade [Year 4] and remained static between fourth and fifth grades [Years 5 and 6].' As well as fearlessly generating significant numbers of ideas in Years 4 and 5, students' scores for originality are also very high: 'until fifth grade, children [are] increasingly open-minded and curious and more apt to produce unique responses'. However, Kim found that 'creative' responses subsequently drop off. Idea production

---

42 Bayles and Orland, *Art and Fear*, p. 27.
43 Bayles and Orland, *Art and Fear*, p. 26.

'then continuously decreased, which might indicate children become alert to issues like accuracy and appropriateness of their responses when they generate ideas'.[44]

When Pablo Picasso famously said, 'All children are artists,' he was right. Sadly he was perhaps also right when he suggested, 'The problem is how to *stay* an artist.'[45]

Brené Brown, research professor at the University of Houston, has amassed a vast number of interviews in her research on people's experiences of empathy, courage and shame. She finds that about a third of people can recall what she calls a 'creativity scar' – a defining event when their creative endeavours were criticised or their talent called into question.[46] Of course the impact of an event like this can be profound. Many years after the events of our childhood we still both wince at specific memories of poorly executed stories or early attempts at fiction. We're going back an alarming number of years now, but our teachers' use of the word 'natural' to describe creative talent had a pervasive effect, particularly when it wasn't applied to us. It's no wonder that some students opt out of being creative.

Any manifesto should encourage students to opt back in.

So that's our creative manifesto. It's a position and viewpoint we've argued passionately and consistently with classes, and with patience and persistence it's one that's worked. There are lots of ways in which this might become a checklist of behaviours, a list of short quotes, a roll call of characteristics to share with aspiring writers – do with it what you want!

---

44 Kyung Hee Kim, 'The Creativity Crisis: The Decrease in Creative Thinking Scores on the Torrance Tests of Creative Thinking', *Creativity Research Journal* 23(4) (2011): 285–295 at p. 291.

45 See Laurence J. Peter, *Peter's Quotations: Ideas for Our Time* (New York: Bantam Books, 1977), p. 25.

46 Brené Brown, *Daring Greatly: How the Courage to Be Vulnerable Transforms the Way We Live, Love, Parent, and Lead* (London: Penguin, 2013).

CHAPTER 2

FORGE-ING STRATEGIES

This chapter of *Storycraft* will suggest ten strategies for creating an abundance of micro-ideas for potential stories. The aim is to create a wealth of possibilities so that students can be flexible, resilient and creative in the face of any potential project or exam question.

As we mentioned in the previous chapter, it's important to explore the notion of micro-ideas with your students. We're not looking for fully formed story ideas here; we're collecting the individual components that will help us to craft stories at a later date. The outcomes of these activities will be scribbled notes, lists of possibilities, observations and potential story ideas. As a result, it might be appropriate to design a space for collecting the outcomes of these activities. Each student might have a journal or notebook. They might be submitting anonymised ideas on flash cards. There might be a collective online document where ideas are amassed. We're fond of torn-off strips of paper folded up and dropped into a tray, then randomly withdrawn again.

The activities are structured and reasonably formal: you might want to try a few in class, give one or two as homework or use them as a menu of options for students. The gathering of the outcomes is up to you. These tasks won't generate stories, but rather the seeds of stories, so you needn't worry about huge piles of marking.

There are a number of principles that we think are important to emphasise during the pre-production phase of the creative process:

- Long thinking means accumulating and keeping hold of ideas over a sustained period. There is no 'best before' date on ideas. Record them and sift through them after they've had time to gestate. Activities like Thirty-One Elevator Pitches (Activity 2), Person, Place, Problem (Activity 9) or Hearts and Clubs (Activity 10) can be returned to again and again, and should become a habitual part of idea generation.

- Quantity beats quality. If one in three micro-ideas will be potentially good, we need 300 of them in order to have 100 interesting components to play with: aim for lots and lots of bad ideas and the good ideas will follow. Often our early ideas are uninspiring or derivative, so we need to get beyond them. The Cycle Courier Challenge (Activity 1) will help to illustrate this point.

- It only takes a moment to record an idea. Gather everything, no matter how small or seemingly insignificant.

- The dreamer must beat the critic in this phase of creativity. We should aim to generate ideas free from the practical concerns that might accompany actually using them. No need to shoot down ideas because they don't make sense or they would be difficult to pull off. Title Race (Activity 3) generates lots of ideas precisely because the students don't have to write the story they're speculating about.

- Combinations of ideas emerge when we observe, record, research and experiment. An idea in and of itself might appear uninteresting, but in combination with three or four others it might explode into life.

Hopefully the activities here will be useful in creating an array of possibilities, all of which can be carried into the activities in the chapters that follow.

ACTIVITY 1. THE CYCLE COURIER CHALLENGE

In this activity, your job is to list ideas in response to a scenario that's given below. We're going to ask you for ten of them. Before you read the scenario, though, here's what we're interested in: *seeing when your best and most original ideas emerge.* Is your first idea your favourite? Or is it the second or third? Is your tenth idea your most original? Or are all of them, in your opinion, terrible?

As you list your ideas you must do it chronologically – in the order you get them. Be completely uncritical. If a bad idea springs to mind, record it. If all ten are bad in your opinion, that's fine.

OK, now for the scenario. Think of the cycle couriers you see in towns and cities. They usually zoom around on their bikes weaving in and out of traffic. Their bikes have large cube-shaped delivery boxes on them, usually because they're ferrying takeaway food like pizza.

Now consider this: what if every cycle courier in your nearest town or city looked as if they were delivering fast food, but really it was a disguise and they were delivering something else entirely? What could the something else be?

Right, you're off. Make a list of possibilities below:

1. ....

2. ....

3. ....

4. ....

5. ....

6. ....

7. ....

8. ....

9. ....

10. ....

Now that you've made your list you might want to consider the following:

▪ Give every idea a score between 1 and 5 (with 1 being 'common' and 5 being 'most creative'). Then design and plot a simple graph to illustrate where your good ideas came – early, late or somewhere in the middle.

▪ Choose your favourite idea – the one you consider the best and most original. Then pick your least exciting idea. Where did the best and worst ideas come in the process?

These two activities should give you a chance to reflect on when your best ideas come – straightaway or with persistence.

Now have a look at the following table. It represents three other people responding to the Cycle Courier Challenge:

Person 1		Person 2		Person 3	
1	Guns	1	Biological weapons	1	Drugs
2	Poisonous liquids	2	Bombs	2	Illegal weapons
3	Party cakes	3	Sandwiches	3	Animals
4	Smuggled pets	4	Water	4	Explosives
5	Bricks	5	Ribbons	5	Plans to create destruction
6	Chopped-off heads	6	Rabbits/pets	6	Diamonds

ACTIVITY 1

Person 1		Person 2		Person 3	
7	Stakes for killing vampires	7	Library books that are late	7	Shoes
8	Doorways to other worlds	8	Swimwear	8	Passports
9	Universes	9	Fluff	9	Bacon
10	A very slow prison break – one limb at a time	10	Ideas	10	Babies

Look for patterns in the responses. You might want to consider choosing one of the following investigations:

1. Call answers 1–4 'early answers'. What are the characteristics of early answers? What ideas do our imaginations generate at the beginning of a challenge?

   Look out for the 'drugs-guns-bombs' answers. These always come up. Everyone thinks of them because the movies, TV thrillers and computer games of our society always use them. There's an important lesson here: if you choose to go with your first idea, there's a good chance it will be everyone else's first idea too.

   Answers 5–7 are 'middle answers' and answers 8–10 are 'late answers'. Are there particular characteristics of answers as the challenge goes on? Where are the best answers most commonly found in your opinion? Are there exceptions to this?

2. Why are the good ideas good? Collect the answers you consider to be the best – it doesn't matter where they appear. Then try to describe why they are successful.

3. What characterises the weaker ideas? Collect together all the ideas that seem familiar, dull or uninteresting. Why don't they work?

4. Generate a list of rules for yourself about idea generation. When do your best ideas come? What must you do more of when trying to develop ideas? What must you do less of?

ACTIVITY 2. THIRTY-ONE ELEVATOR PITCHES TO FEED CREATIVITY

When an author has to sell a story fast they use an elevator pitch. This means telling the outline story in two or three sentences. (It's meant to be so quick that you could meet a famous film-maker in an elevator and summarise your fantastic story before they have a chance to escape!) In the case of films, the shorter the pitch, the stronger the idea:

- *Jaws*: A police chief with a fear of water faces a giant man-eating shark that is terrorising a busy holiday resort.

- *The Hunger Games*: Poor people fight each other to entertain the rich. One girl stands up to them and leads a rebellion.

- *Romeo and Juliet*: Two young lovers from feuding families marry in secret and get separated with tragic results.

- *The Matrix*: An office worker and computer hacker discovers the truth of human existence – we are all enslaved and asleep.

- *Harry Potter and the Philosopher's Stone*: An orphaned boy discovers he's a wizard, and is enrolled at wizarding school, where he uncovers a plot to hide a magical item.

What follows is a table of thirty-one suggestions or prompts that might relate to an object, a type of person, an animal, a place or the weather. See what micro-ideas these suggestions generate. Think about where the story might take place. Then add a character, imagine a haunting image and build the opening to a film in your mind.

Each week, spend ten or fifteen minutes thinking of a story idea using one of the prompts. Do this by jotting down as many ideas as you can. They can be silly or sensible – it doesn't matter. You can use the words in the table as an inspiration or as a title. There must be some kind of link, even if it's quite tenuous. Then, once you've done some thinking, try to sum your story up as an elevator pitch: you have three sentences or fewer. (Some of your pitches will end up better than others – and that doesn't matter!)

For example, you might be given 'A food blender'. You start to list some ideas:

- An accident needs clearing up.
- Somebody prepares a meal for a mixed group of people who are antagonistic towards each other.
- Somebody kills people and blends their remains into food and sells it.
- An argument between two very different people in a kitchen.
- A rogue asparagus spear leads a revolution against a chef and kills him, aided by a psychotic sausage who stuffs the chef into the blender.
- A woman is preparing for a dinner party but is also planning to poison her husband.
- A man is preparing a birthday meal for his wife and remembering the day his hamster fell into the food blender … or did he put it there himself?
- A woman is preparing food in the kitchen while also preparing to propose to her girlfriend.

You might not be happy with them all – you'll know that some are better than others. You pick one. Maybe you quite like the argument because it has lots of conflict. But then you think of the woman poisoning her husband and the story you could tell. You could make it sound like she really cares about him and finish with her sprinkling the poison into two dishes, his and the woman he's cheated with. The final line might be something like 'That's why they have to die.'

The pitch might be: 'A woman prepares a meal and thinks of all the reasons she loves her husband. Then she sprinkles poison on his food because he has cheated on her.' You could even boil it down to: 'An angry wife prepares a poisoned meal for her husband and his mistress.'

OK, here are your starting points:

1	The tunnel and the lamp
2	The nightshift

3	The dying lion
4	A yellow Rolls-Royce
5	The surgeon
6	The empty shopping centre
7	The caged parrot
8	The locked toolbox
9	An unopened letter
10	The priest with bad dreams
11	The lost passport
12	A beach in winter
13	The railway guard
14	An unexpected heatwave
15	The addict
16	The silk scarf
17	A lighthouse in a storm
18	The wolf pack
19	The mystical detective
20	A lost mobile phone

21	A suitcase in the woods
22	A message in spray paint
23	A pampered cat
24	A checkout girl with tattoos
25	A forest at night
26	Something buried
27	Walking boots with missing laces
28	A cracked photograph
29	The judge
30	A slowly roasting chicken
31	Burning papers

There are thirty-one ideas here, but if you want a quick start you can pick the idea that represents the date of your birth or the month in which you were born, just to see what ideas emerge. You could even do one of these a day for a whole month, though you might try this in February!

Try creating your own lists too!

ACTIVITY 2

ACTIVITY 3. TITLE RACE

For some authors, titles are a nightmare, only thought about after the book is written. F. Scott Fitzgerald had numerous titles for his novel *The Great Gatsby* and tried to change it almost as the book went to the printers. Other authors might find the title a useful starting point. Sometimes a word or a phrase can inspire a story.

Jon's award-winning book *The Demon Collector* began from the title. We imagine that *Murder on the Orient Express* was firmly in Agatha Christie's mind when she wrote about a murder … on the Orient Express.

Obviously, there are an infinite number of titles and covering every type would be unhelpful. Many titles don't always inspire, or they leave us adrift with an idea that is too general for a short, punchy piece. Other titles are ideal for interrogating and developing ideas.

Here are just a few activities based around titles which might jump-start your creative thinking.

The Last …

Stories about the last in the line of something are often poignant and powerful: *The Last Samurai*, *The Last Wild*, *The Last Wolf*, *The Last Jedi*. They can be about nature or rites of passage, or they can be thought-provoking by using seemingly everyday items, professions or events: The Last Christmas, The Last Summer, The Last Automobile, The Last Hairdresser, The Last Goodbye.

… At the End of the World

Similarly, add a profession, type of shop or entertainment venue to 'at the end of the world' and you get an interesting starting point: The Cafe at the End of the World, The Nail Bar at the End of the World, The Supermarket at the End of the World. Perhaps the Plumber at the End of the World, or add another location to get The Station at the End of the World, The Castle at the End of the World or The Island at the End of the World.

Try 'edge' instead of 'end' and see if it alters the feel or generates some new ideas.

The Empty …

Rather like 'The Last', just choose a noun and put it after 'The Empty'. It could be a location like a beach or school. It could be an object such as a cup, bottle, shoe or suitcase. It could be an abstract idea: The Empty Promise, for example. Certain types of person work quite well too: The Empty Child or simply Empty Man.

The Something in or on the Something

The Girl on the Train springs to mind! Philip Pullman titled four books using this method, starting with *The Ruby in the Smoke*. This title pattern can be adapted to different genres quite easily: The Face in the Mirror sounds creepy, while The Girl in the Dream sounds more romantic.

The Something of …

This is a classic for serial action adventures and fantasy, as well as a favourite of the Star Wars franchise – think *The Return of the Jedi* – or Tolkien's *The Return of the King*. Use objects to get titles like The Sword of …, The Poisoned Arrows of … or The Lake of … Throw in an abstract idea to get The Island of Hope or The Dagger of Forgetting. Make it comic by combining silly things: The Mantelpiece of Terror or The Curtains of Suspicion. Add a character name to get *Harry Potter and the Chamber of Secrets* or *Indiana Jones and the Temple of Doom.*

The Kitten Slayer

Finally, random combinations often work. The following table has two columns. Pick a word from each and create your own story. You'll notice that some of the combinations are bizarre, so you should not take the titles too literally. Think of the associations with each word – for example, 'kitten' might bring to mind weakness, playfulness, vulnerability or cuteness. A wrestler doesn't necessarily have to be a person who physically fights an opponent; it might mean someone coping with a lot of demands all at once or someone facing a physical challenge. On the other hand, the Scrapyard Strangler might just be that! And the Five-Dollar Juggler might be about someone on low wages who is struggling to make ends meet.

Kitten	Whisperer
Mannequin	Destroyer
Knife	Kidnapper
Fridge Magnet	Chaser
Tree	Rescuer
Skateboard	Stealer
Dragon	Smuggler
Ten-Pin Skittle	Wrestler
Carpet	Strangler
Scrapyard	Murderer
Machine Gun	Seller
North Star	Collector
Button	Driver
Five-Dollar	Dreamer
Elevator	Juggler

ACTIVITY 4. THIRTY PROVERBS AND SAYINGS

Proverbs get us thinking because there's often a lot of wisdom packed into a very small saying. It gives us the chance to begin to think beyond the literal. Here's an example: 'Too many cooks spoil the broth.'

This can be read literally – you could write a short narrative set in a kitchen – but it might not be the most inspiring piece. Instead, you might consider the message that proverbs are trying to convey. They're essentially metaphors for much more complicated ideas, usually some sort of warning about behaviour. This can make them difficult to understand: often when you read a proverb for the first time, you need to really think about it before its full meaning becomes clear.

But that thinking will be worth it! By prohibiting the obvious literal interpretation of the proverb, we can encourage some much more interesting ideas. As you consider the following list, collect any connotations, associations or characters they bring to mind. Choose or randomly select one of the thirty proverbs and:

- Write a short description of a character inspired by the proverb.

- Write a short piece in which the character demonstrates those characteristics.

- Plan a story that ends with one of the proverbs.

1	Fire is a good servant but a bad master.
2	Dogs wag their tails not so much for you as for your food.
3	Every horse thinks its own pack the heaviest.
4	Misery loves company.
5	The grass is always greener on the other side.
6	A bad workman blames his tools.
7	Hope for the best, prepare for the worst.

8	Those who make no mistakes make nothing.
9	Lightning never strikes twice in the same place.
10	Don't get mad, get even.
11	It is better to be the hammer than the nail.
12	Keep your friends close and your enemies closer.
13	A beggar can never be bankrupt.
14	Better the devil you know than the devil you don't.
15	Fortune favours the brave.
16	Revenge is a dish best served cold.
17	Two wrongs don't make a right.
18	It's the squeaking wheel that gets the oil.
19	A rich man's joke always gets a laugh.
20	If you pay peanuts, you'll get monkeys.
21	Those who do not learn from history are doomed to repeat it.
22	If you play with fire, you'll get burned.
23	The chain breaks where it is weakest.
24	Strike while the iron is hot.
25	In the kingdom of the blind, the one-eyed man is king.

26	A fool and their money are soon parted.
27	All that glitters is not gold.
28	My enemy's enemy is my friend.
29	Rob Peter to pay Paul.
30	Never bite the hand that feeds you.

ACTIVITY 4

ACTIVITY 5. INVERSIONS, UPDATES, REWRITES, MASH-UPS AND MINOR CHARACTERS

Imagine if children were in charge of society and adults had to do as they were told. That's an inversion. Imagine if Little Red Riding Hood was the predator and hunted the wolf. That's an inversion too.

At a simple level inversions can be used to create new takes on old classics: The Three Little Wolves and the Big Bad Pig, for example.

Another example inversion is the Noughts and Crosses series by Malorie Blackman, which envisages an alternate reality in which the privileges of race are switched and a white population lives in a segregated society that discriminates against them. This more complex form of inversion requires more thought and research but could yield exciting results. Readers love alternate worlds that are similar to their own.

- **Classic inversions**: Choose a fairy tale and reverse the roles – make the heroes of the story into villains and vice versa.

- **Historic inversions**: This is used to create a world for the story. Imagine an event in history, perhaps a battle or war, and flip it. A good example is if the Nazi regime in 1940s Germany had won the Second World War. This is the premise of several TV series and the Carnegie Medal-winning novel *Maggot Moon* by Sally Gardner.

- **Power inversions**: Who holds the power? Who makes the rules? Flip it. The day the schoolchildren took over, or suddenly pets are in charge.

- **Gender inversions**: Great for puncturing classic gender stereotypes.

- **Climate inversions**: Again, good for settings. Imagine the United Kingdom as arid desert. How did it get like that? What is society like now?

- **Character inversions**: Characters that we normally imagine to be good turn out to be evil and vice versa. Rather like classic inversions but with just one character rather than the whole story. This could be a sadistic doctor or a kind vampire.

UPDATES AND REWRITES

In Martin's novel *Payback*, he began by thinking about what Robin Hood might look like as a story if we tried updating it and setting it today. A number of exciting ideas emerged: Robin Hood might be a gang of teenagers, not one person. They might fight evil corporations and corrupt companies instead of a greedy royal family. They might be urban rather than rural … and so on.

What if we tried to retell the story of Cinderella? First, we'd need to get to the heart of the story. Have a think about the following:

- What is it really about?

- What are its themes and ideas?

- What is the story for? What is it telling us?

- What are the things we couldn't remove without breaking it?

Now consider this: which bits could we change to make it more relevant? Think about the settings, characters and main events. Then consider these challenges:

- Swap the gender of the key characters and see what happens.

- Remove the slipper – then make a list of ten objects or ideas which could replace the slipper and make the story more interesting or unusual.

- Swap the number of characters. One ugly sister and three Cinderellas – how would that work? Explore it further.

- Give Cinderella the magic and remove the fairy godmother.

- Set it in a boarding school, on a cruise ship, in a prison or prisoner-of-war camp … List another ten options here.

- Combine the fairy godmother and one of the ugly sisters (or brothers). How would that affect things?

- Remove royalty and replace it with some other type of power or status.

Now consider other stories and experiment with them:

- Fairy tales.

- Childhood stories.
- The last book you read.
- Favourite films.

MASH-UPS: CINDERELLA MEETS THE WALKING DEAD

Another way to use familiar material is to crash two unexpected genres head-on. The example we've given here is, on the one hand, crazy, but on the other, it might make you suddenly consider things differently. (Are the ugly sisters ugly because they're zombies?)

One way you can shake up your thinking and collect ideas is to try some of these mash-ups. Make a list of thirty novels, comics, TV shows or movies. Write each one on a sticky note, fold it up and put it in a container. Then randomly pull them out, seeing if you can crash two of them together in an arresting and unusual way.

MINOR CHARACTERS TAKING CENTRE STAGE

One of the stories most English students end up reading at some point in their school career is Louis Sachar's *Holes*. It's a brilliant novel filled with wonderful characters. Most people have either read *Holes* or seen the movie version, and most people can remember the main characters. Some recall Mr Sir, the strict disciplinarian who runs the prison camp for tearaway boys. Others remember the first time we encounter the Warden. Others remember Stanley or Zero with great fondness, or the Wild West outlaw Kissin' Kate Barlow.

Here's a character we're a little obsessed with: the car thief called Twitch. Twitch only turns up towards the end of the book. He really only appears in one important scene – helping to steal Mr Sir's truck. Then he drifts into the background and we don't see much of him again.

What if we tried to write Twitch's story?

Choosing a minor character and putting them centre stage is a really useful way to get your ideas going. Every character considers themselves the hero of their own story; in this activity you get the chance to make an underappreciated character the protagonist for once!

Make a list of minor characters you might consider.

ACTIVITY 6. TWENTY-MINUTE MOVIE FEED

For this activity you'll need a stopwatch, a notebook and a movie to watch. It can be anything you like.

OK, let's start with the maths. An average movie is about 120 minutes long. Usually we find we can tell whether we want to watch any further after about twenty minutes – in other words, less than 20% of the way through. It's worth thinking about this yourself: when do you instinctively know when you're going to like something or not? You might watch for a little bit, telling yourself to give it a chance, but eventually you know the story isn't going to interest you.

For us, twenty minutes tells us everything we need to know. If we're enjoying it, twenty minutes is the point at which we know we're totally aligned with the world of the story, the motivation of the characters, the direction of travel, the mood and theme – and we're going to follow it all the way to the end.

Try watching the first twenty minutes of any movie you like with a stopwatch. Get the credits out of the way before you start the clock, unless the story begins immediately. Then jot down what you know by the end of the first twenty minutes. Make notes under the following headings:

- **Protagonist**: Who is/are the main character/s? What do they want? What motivates them? How do we know?

- **The world**: Where is the story set? What is 'normal' in this world? How do we know?

- **Antagonist**: What is stopping the protagonist getting what they want? Is it a person, idea, place or thing?

- **Themes**: What key ideas are emerging? What does the story seem to be about?

Here are three examples from our own notes, getting more contemporary as they go on:

- ***Signs* (M. Night Shyamalan, 2002)**

  We are introduced to an ex-priest living on a farm surrounded by acres of deep corn fields. Strange stuff is happening and his kids are noticing it. The water tastes odd. The dog's going bonkers. There's something out in the fields, and we soon learn that it's responsible for the appearance of a massive crop circle.

The cops come to investigate. The main character (played by Mel Gibson) is a priest with a tragic past who seems to have lost his faith in God. He says, 'Don't call me "Father".' The following night there's another intruder on the farm – unidentified. Crop circles are turning up all over the world according to the TV news. The cops return.

At twenty minutes: the characters, location and situation have all been introduced. The main characters begin investigating the strange phenomena.

The Ghost Writer (Roman Polanski, 2010)

The opening scene is on a ferry. An abandoned car is towed away after the ferry docks at Vineyard Haven. The body of its driver is washed up on a nearby beach. Maybe the victim has committed suicide or maybe he's been thrown off the boat. Cut to London: a writer (Ewan McGregor) chats with his agent about a potentially exciting new job – ghostwriting the ex-prime minister's autobiography. He gets the gig, flies to New York and travels out to Martha's Vineyard, the scene of the ferry death we saw at the start. Could there be a connection with the ferry death and the job he's just taken?

At exactly twenty minutes: he steps out of the back of a cab after a punishing sixteen-hour journey, ready to start his new assignment.

The Rim of the World (Joseph Nicol, 2019)

We get an introduction to a nerdy, computer-obsessed indoorsy kid called Alex. He's intelligent, introverted and excellent with a Rubik's cube. His mum is forcing him to go to summer camp – a place called Rim of the World – because she's worried that he hasn't got any friends.

We watch his mum drop him off. We are introduced to some of the comedy characters at the camp. Alex finds the activities difficult and has to climb down from the high zip wire. We get hints that his father may have died in a fire. Alex meets three other characters with whom he becomes friends.

At twenty minutes: the four friends find themselves suddenly alone, separated from the rest of the camp. Shock and disbelief as they discover something life-changing: aliens are attacking the Earth.

Twenty minutes certainly seems to be the point, in a 120-minute movie, at which everything is established and the story is ready to go.

Gather anything that has interested you during the experiment. There might be a character tic, an interesting line of dialogue, a scene, a situation or an idea for the beginning of a story of your own.

Generate a list of ingredients that make the perfect first twenty minutes of a movie.

ACTIVITY 7. WHAT IF? VS. WHAT WOULD YOU DO IF?

WHAT IF?

Ask any author about starting a story and they might tell you that a good place to start is asking the question, 'what if?' There's a long and successful history of writers playing with what ifs in order to generate story ideas, particularly if your what if encourages further ideas about what your world might be like.

Let's hear two writers talk about what ifs. One is the horror writer Stephen King:

> The most interesting situations can usually be expressed as a What-if question.[1]

The other is comic-fantasy novelist Terry Pratchett:

> You are allowed to make pigs fly, but you must take into account the need for people in heavily over-flown areas to carry stout umbrellas at all times.[2]

The aim of the what if is to open your mind to new possibilities. Here are ten what ifs:

	What if ...
1	A disturbance in the Earth's orbit meant gravity was going to vanish for an hour and we knew exactly when?
2	Certain types of people never needed to sleep?
3	The birth rate dropped so that almost no children were being born?

---

1   Stephen King, *On Writing: A Memoir of the Craft* (New York: Simon & Schuster, 2000), p. 196.
2   Terry Pratchett, 'Notes from a Successful Fantasy Author: Keep It Real', in *A Slip of the Keyboard: Collected Non-Fiction* (London: Corgi, 2015), p. 85.

	What if ...
4	The country's leaders had to be younger than twenty and were selected following a nationwide exam?
5	Certain people were resistant to every disease on the planet?
6	You won the National Lottery?
7	A rebellious group of students took over the running of a school?
8	Unicorns really existed?
9	Other animals could talk?
10	The Nazis had won the Second World War?

It is not a bad way to start, but it is limited and problematic as a springboard for short fiction. The question only really sets a context for the broadest of possibilities and doesn't give us a clear idea about how to start a story. Like this: 'What if I won the National Lottery? I'd be rich!' There doesn't seem to be a great story there – it requires a lot of extra thinking.

Let's try another: 'What if other animals could talk?'

You need to drill down into it to get the best ideas: animals could ask for food, they could complain about their lives, they could spread gossip, they may be witnesses to crimes. Once you have these possibilities you have to ask more questions: would some animals just complain all the time? Would they have realistic expectations? Would they be trustworthy? Would some animals be more reliable than others? Would cats be more likely to lie than dogs? Could a human be convicted on evidence provided by a house sparrow?

This in turn opens up other possibilities: if a human could be convicted on the evidence of a house sparrow, would we use them as a police force, spying on the population and gathering information? Would humans begin to mistrust certain animals?

These are all fun considerations, great for in-depth world-building and fertile ground for a lengthy piece of work – but for fast, short-form writing, which is what most often happens in a classroom, maybe the what if question is too broad.

WHAT WOULD YOU DO IF?

What ifs are all very well, but we've found that ideas often come more quickly, and are of a higher quality, if you use the question, 'What would you do if?'

It has three advantages over the more general question. First, it places you at the heart of the question, making you the narrator of a potential story. Second, it provokes an active response. If you won the National Lottery what would you *do*? Buy a Ferrari? Give the money away? The story has begun already. Third, it often places the writer in a ready-made dilemma.

All the writer has to do now is to think of a few pitfalls associated with their situation. We have found that three supplementary questions are enough to get writing:

1. What would be the best thing(s) associated with this event?

2. What would be the worst thing(s) associated with this event?

3. Which person you thought you could trust would let you down because of this event?

These questions set up two main parts of the story: the set-up and the betrayal. They also guide the writer to think of a problem that will make their writing interesting. So, instead of, 'What if animals could talk?' you might want to ask, 'What would you do if your cat started talking to you?' Quickly jot down what might be good about this and also who might betray you.

The response might be as follows:

■ **What would you do if your cat started talking to you?** I might wonder if I was going mad. I might ask what it thinks about its life.

■ **What would be the best things about your cat being able to talk?** You could frighten friends. The cat could spy for you. It might be wise and clever.

■ **What would be the worst things about your cat being able to talk?** The cat might give away personal secrets. Adults might be interested in it and want to experiment on it or weaponise it. The cat might start making unreasonable demands.

■ **Which person you thought you could trust would let you down because of this event?** My best friend because she might get jealous and tell everyone. Then the cat would become a celebrity or even a scientific specimen!

It's important to note that the person letting you down doesn't always have to do it for bad reasons; if your mother discovered you were talking to the cat, she might suggest a trip to the doctor or a psychiatrist. She would be acting in what she saw as your best interests. Often, the best villains are the ones who are convinced they are doing good.

Note: Trying to keep something secret often makes betrayal easier and raises the tension in the story. Most dilemma situations lend themselves to secrets and betrayals.

Try placing yourself in the following 'What would you do if?' situations. Choose or randomly select one of the situations and then use the three questions above to build up some ideas for your story:

	What would you do if ...
1	You suddenly discovered that your pet could talk?
2	You found a suitcase full of money hidden on some wasteland?
3	Following an accident you discovered that you could read minds?
4	You found a diary from the future that listed upcoming sports results, political events and major disasters?

	What would you do if ...
5	You found a small but perfectly formed unicorn in your back garden?
6	You found a winning National Lottery ticket but weren't old enough to cash it?
7	You found out that your new teacher used to be a hitman and is on the run from the Mob?
8	You overheard a friend planning to run away from an abusive parent or guardian?
9	You found alien technology that made you super-intelligent?
10	You were a witness to a corner shop robbery and knew the thieves?

ACTIVITY 7

ACTIVITY 8. SHOULD I OR SHOULDN'T I?

A dilemma is a situation in which the main character has to make a choice. These can be earth-shattering (in order to save the human race I have to kill my own brother) or they can be more domestic (should I break my friend's trust and tell an adult her secret for her own good?).

Dilemma situations are great because they draw the reader in and make them think about what they would do. The character is in a tricky situation because they have a difficult decision to make.

Here are a few dilemmas:

- Your best friend is self-harming. Only you know. Do you tell someone?

- Someone has a photograph of you at a party when you told your parents you were studying at a friend's house. They blackmail you into doing something.

- You have a chance to audition for a band and have a good chance of success. But it's your best friend's birthday party and she won't understand.

- A boy in your class has learning difficulties and is being bullied by some other students. You are afraid to confront them because they used to pick on you.

- You are out with your friends when you see a happily married relative apparently having a romantic meal with a stranger. The relative sees you and begs you not to say anything.

Remember, in the best stories characters always make bad choices! We might anguish over some of these situations but we would probably seek advice. However, your character needs to make the wrong choice and then try to patch it up. How easy that is depends on how long your story is and how much mental anguish you want to put your character through. You can also complicate the situation:

What would you do if you found an old woman lying unconscious in the street?

With fifty pounds poking out of her pocket.

Two twenties and a ten.

Obviously, you would call the emergency services to help her. If you wanted to create an interesting story, then your character has to make the wrong choice. Perhaps they take the money or some of it. There's nobody around. She doesn't know what's happening. Anyone who passed by could have taken it. Anyway, the old woman will probably be in hospital for a while so she isn't going to need it. Perhaps the character takes the money to keep it safe and then encounters another situation in which fifty pounds will solve the problem. One dilemma can follow another. Should I keep the money or give it to my mum so she can stop the loan shark from taking the TV?

Following one dilemma with another is easy with money-related stories but it can work with relationships too:

> Character A is asked to keep a secret by character B.
>
> Character A worries about keeping the secret.
>
> Then someone close to character B confides that they are worried about them and character A betrays the secret.
>
> Then character B finds out character A has betrayed them.
>
> There's trouble!

These dilemmas can occur as a subplot in longer fiction but would probably be the main story in shorter work.

ALIEN VAMPIRES: ADDING A TWIST

A twist is when something unexpected arises out of the narrative. The clues are usually there but the reader has been misdirected by the narrator. Sometimes, dilemmas and 'what would you do if?' questions allow room for a twist in your story. Some twists come out of the blue and are totally unexpected, but these can feel artificial and contrived if they haven't grown out of the actual story. For example, if the unconscious old woman turned out to be an alien vampire who leapt up and killed the protagonist with no warning, that wouldn't be very satisfying. However, if the narrator had described the old woman's appearance as odd and maybe mentioned strange lights in the sky the night before, then the possibility of alien vampires has been seeded in the reader's mind. It is always

ACTIVITY 8

better to leave some clues as to what the twist might be; in this way, the reader will find it more satisfying.

A classic twist is that the motives of the narrator aren't what the reader assumed. For example, the main character considers saving the old woman, and the reader fully expects her to do so, but in the end she walks off with the money. Or maybe she turns out to be a mugger who has returned to her victim after first running away in fear of being caught. Perhaps the narrator paid someone to kill the old woman and she has come to check she is dead.

Sometimes the object of the dilemma might provide the twist: the old woman might be lying in wait to test the honesty of passers-by as part of some TV prank programme. It may be the relationship between the object of the dilemma and the narrator that provides the twist: the old woman may be known or related to the narrator.

A twist could be an unexpected turn of events and how the narrator reacts to them. This still requires a link to the narrative though: having a character struck by lightning won't work unless the character, having deliberated over robbing the old woman, thinks: 'It's not as if God will strike me down!'

If, as in the suggestion in the table in Activity 7, you discovered your pet could talk, it would be interesting if the cat or dog in question started blackmailing you.

A story doesn't have to have a twist but if you can think of one, it's satisfying for the reader.

ACTIVITY 9. PERSON, PLACE, PROBLEM

There are two approaches to this activity. The first will push your imagination to make connections and might feel a little uncomfortable. The second gives you a greater element of control. Your aim in each activity is to kick-start a story from unfamiliar or unusual ingredients. There may well be some illogical contrasts to deal with along the way.

In this activity you're going to get a person (a character), a place to put them in and a problem that they have. Your task is to use the three elements to conjure up a possible story – and then begin writing it.

VERSION 1:

Choose three random numbers between 1 and 20. They can be the same number repeated three times or any sequence of numbers you want.

Your first number will give you a person. Check the person grid that follows, find the number you've chosen and make a note of the random person you've been assigned.

Your second number will give you a place. Check the place grid, find the number you've chosen and make a note of the random place you've been assigned. Your person must be here as the story starts.

Your third number will give you a problem. Check the problem grid, find the number you've chosen and make a note of the random problem you've been assigned. These are deliberately vague to give you some room to adjust and adapt.

The random combination of three things should give you a bit of a headache – so spend some time sitting with it and bringing the story to life!

VERSION 2:

Scan the three grids and choose your favourites – one person, one place and one problem.

The results should be a little more predictable, but again you'll need to spend some time stitching it all together and figuring out how the story works.

Look overleaf for your grids.

Person:

1. A paperboy with a broken bike he found or stole.	2. Twins who think the same thoughts even when they're apart.	3. A kid who's just had a secret tattoo done.	4. A boy dressed as Anna from *Frozen* with a rucksack full of cash.
5. A schoolchild haunted by bad dreams featuring a stranger.	6. The worst goalkeeper ever – convinced they're cursed.	7. A young boy/girl who can't sleep walks the streets at night.	8. A girl, an ex-school Frisbee champion, who is now in disgrace.
9. A piano player with a missing finger.	10. A kid who writes made-up horoscopes for the school magazine.	11. A student trying to make the scariest movie ever on their iPhone.	12. A chocolate maker with a valuable secret recipe.
13. A taxi driver, new in the city, on their first night's work.	14. A part-time hotel porter who disturbs a break-in.	15. Two children, bags of supplies packed, set out to go fishing on their secret lake.	16. A bad magician who's convinced they're actually really good.
17. A schoolchild who discovers their teacher is a former MI6 assassin.	18. Two brothers, one cheerful and the other gloomy.	19. A student with a violin they found abandoned on the bus.	20. Someone with a special pack of playing cards.

Place:

1. Waking up in a hospital bed behind a drawn curtain.	2. A train station at midnight, with the last train just pulling in.	3. An abandoned alleyway in the city centre.	4. Outside some run-down changing rooms at an old boxing club.
5. In an empty candle-lit room with the table laid for dinner for three.	6. Stepping down the stairs towards the cellar with a torch.	7. Opening a trapdoor into the loft for the first time.	8. Totally distracted and getting off a bus at the wrong stop.
9. An aircraft hangar, empty and echoey, with a car parked in the middle.	10. A jetty extending twenty feet out into a huge muddy river.	11. The centre of a bridge over a railway line.	12. Riding a skateboard across an empty car park at 2am, heading for school.
13. Sheltering from the rain in the porch of an old church.	14. On the muddiest football pitch ever, with rain lashing down.	15. Heading away from the beach and pushing into the jungle.	16. Under someone else's desk, looking for a lost item.
17. Trying to climb a high fence for a bet.	18. Looking down a deep well, eyes caught by a glint in the dark.	19. Having a picnic miles from anywhere, with no phone signal.	20. Counting up stolen apples in the back of a white van.

ACTIVITY 9

Problem:

1. A figure appears – someone not seen for many years.	2. A discarded passport. It belongs to a stranger but the photo ID looks exactly like you …	3. You're asked to look after something. 'Just for a few days,' they say …	4. The weather changes suddenly to a storm, and as you run for shelter …
5. In the distance, a column of smoke. You have a bad feeling.	6. The melting snow reveals something that's been there for weeks.	7. A text message from an unknown number: 'I know who did it.'	8. They can't remember anything about yesterday and want your help.
9. A friend shares a secret – then swears you to silence.	10. A box with a plastic seal. No one has ever opened it. The date on it is …	11. There is a sudden extended silence. Then, in the distance, a howl.	12. You agree to swap phones for the day, just to see what happens.
13. A DVD, with a handwritten note: 'Do NOT watch until 2022.'	14. You had always sworn to help them if they needed you. But this latest request is …	15. You swap coats because it's raining. Later, in the pocket you find …	16. The streetlights go out one at a time and leave you in darkness.
17. Something you've hidden well and told no one about has gone.	18. A drink that makes you cleverer – in a can with Chinese lettering on it.	19. You get your phone back and it's fixed. Except it seems different.	20. A clearing in the bushes. Someone's been here, sleeping rough.

ACTIVITY 10. HEARTS AND CLUBS

For this activity you'll need a pack of playing cards. The hearts and clubs need to be retained. The other cards can be set aside for now.

You should have twenty-six cards – thirteen hearts and thirteen clubs.

- Your hearts are going to represent dreams, desires and wishes. You need to create a character with a particular wish or goal – something they are desperate to achieve.

- Your clubs are going to represent obstacles – things your character is clubbed with and beaten down by.

Deal yourself three random hearts and three random clubs, then use the following table to see what you've got.

	Hearts: a dream/desire/wish	Clubs: an obstacle to frustrate or deny them
Ace	A character who must pass an audition, trial or test so they can become a successful singer/actor/footballer/games designer/university student ...	But there are only two days left before an important deadline and they're miles away from getting what they want.
2	A character who has to find their recently vanished friend ...	But they've just woken from an operation and must try to achieve their goal from a hospital bed.
3	A character who must reunite a couple – two people who love each other but have fallen out ...	But an enemy has stolen something crucial and our character must first get it back.

	Hearts: a dream/desire/wish	Clubs: an obstacle to frustrate or deny them
4	A character who must win an election at all costs ...	But the character is terrified of the dark and must at last face this fear.
5	A character who has to recover a lost item before someone finds out it's gone ...	But the character has been trapped somewhere and their first job is to escape.
6	A character who has to prove their innocence after being publicly and falsely accused of something ...	But there is a strict and frightening parent/teacher/authority figure who won't allow this to happen.
7	A character desperate to find out who killed their pet dog ...	But achieving this thing will destroy a friendship forever.
8	A character who wants to pluck up the courage to ask someone out on a date ...	But the character is haunted by bad memories of a terrible accident.
9	A character so in love with a particular photograph/picture/beautiful object that they have to get their hands on it ...	But they haven't got any money and must somehow acquire some.
10	A character who wants to discover who their birth parent might be ...	But there is a big public event with hundreds of guests attending, so security will be really tight.

	Hearts: a dream/desire/wish	Clubs: an obstacle to frustrate or deny them
Jack	A character who wants to recover a secret item they buried when they were younger ...	But in order to achieve their goal they need to go on a long and complicated journey to get to a specific special place.
Queen	A character who needs to admit something to someone important – perhaps a parent, teacher, friend or sibling ...	But they have amnesia and can't remember exactly what it was they needed to do – it only comes back in brief images and memories.
King	A character who desperately needs to hide something so it isn't discovered ...	But they are being followed by a shadowy and mysterious figure who seems to want to do them harm.

Try pairing them up in any way you can. Consider all the possibilities suggested by the scenario – fill in the gaps and make the story yours. Then note down any new ideas or possibilities that arise.

DIAMONDS AND SPADES

If you're looking for an interesting way to prepare for the exam, you might want to construct the remainder of a pack yourself. It could help you to generate entire stories for you to write up. Consider the following:

- Diamonds might be sidekicks and helpers – characters who show up to assist the main character in their quest. They might have comic value or they could be wise old experts, kindly teachers or lifelong loyal friends.

- Spades might be anything else you want to throw in – character names, lines of dialogue, interesting objects or scenes, random micro-ideas or books, an aspect of or a reference to TV shows or movies you've enjoyed.

Try dealing out different numbers of each cards. Two hearts, two clubs, two diamonds and a spade might be enough to generate a story.

ONE FINAL POSSIBILITY

We've done this with the tiles from a game of dominoes (not the pizza!), a Monopoly board and a box of chocolates before. Are there any other games you could adapt to help you create ideas for stories?

CHAPTER 3

CRAFTING CHARACTERS

KILLING THE VANILLA PROTAGONIST

Whether the student chooses the first- or third-person perspective to tell their story, one of the issues we've repeatedly come across is the accidental use of a vanilla protagonist. As in:

> Vanilla protagonist (noun): A leading character in a play, film, novel, etc. who seems to have no character or personality – a cipher or vehicle for action and reaction. 'Blimey. What a vanilla protagonist. They have zero personality.'

It's understandable if students are working at speed and responding to an unfamiliar and challenging task; the easiest thing to do is dispense with the complexities of character. Protagonists without anxieties, concerns, passions, issues or beliefs are easier to shunt through a scene quickly. They respond, often emotionlessly, to events around them like the avatar we might choose in a computer game. (Students who live on a computer-game-only diet often write vanilla protagonists. The games industry even has a name for the trope: the space marine. Squat, bald and wise-cracking, the space marine is easy to animate without hair, easy to voice without character and easy to propel through mindless action without morality or personality.)

Many of the least effective pieces we've seen have involved a potentially interesting plot event rendered lifeless because the central character is a vacuum. Vanilla protagonists are temptingly straightforward to write since they have no personality or past, but they consequently rob everything around them of drama or significance.

How do we tackle this? A simple approach we've used successfully is to summarise what a character wants. Every character wants something – it's the job of the writer to (1) know what it is and (2) prevent the character from getting it in as many ways as possible.

Beginning by figuring out what their characters want allows students to create richer scenes. Fairy tales often explore the idea of wants in a very explicit way, by giving characters the chance to have their wishes come true. You can express a character's wants, wishes and values through the things they carry, the objects they crave or fetishise, or the things they habitually say or do.

Once we know these things we can begin building obstacles. Obstacles mean conflict, and conflict changes characters. Dynamic, changing characters are where all good stories live.

It's worth discussing conflict and character change with your students. Why are we so drawn to conflict? Obviously, any rational person would flee from a war zone, but minor domestic conflicts seem to draw us in. Major crises attract an audience, as long as they're watching from a safe distance. There's a reason why, when there's a pile-up on the southbound carriageway of a motorway, the northbound traffic slows down.

Conflict changes us; we learn from it. Dynamic character change is crucial if we are to avoid the vanilla protagonist. Chuck Wendig's *Damn Fine Story* is a useful, funny and irreverently written guide to storytelling. His take on character change is as follows: 'the best characters end a story changed. They leave a story a somewhat different character from when they entered it'.[1]

This chapter will suggest a number of activities to help your students to produce better characters – characters with goals and characters embroiled in conflict.

---

1   Chuck Wendig, *Damn Fine Story: Mastering the Tools of a Powerful Narrative* (Cincinnati, OH: Writer's Digest Books, 2017), p. 61.

ACTIVITY 11. WISHES, WANTS AND GOALS

Character motivation (noun): The reasons behind a certain character's decisions and behaviour.

If you suddenly had three wishes what would you wish for? Most people say 'more wishes'. Many stories are based on wish fulfilment. It's one of the reasons people read – they enjoy the wealth, bravery, skill, strength or cunning of others through stories. It's no surprise that some of the oldest stories are based around an ordinary person receiving three wishes. It's a really easy way for the writer to indicate what their characters want. And, of course, characters who want something are more interesting!

We are fascinated by the idea of things that are normally hard to achieve or attain coming to us effortlessly through magical means. But the story, as ever, only begins when things go wrong.

There are several ways this can happen:

- **The Midas wish**: In these stories, the character gets exactly what they want but it proves to be more of a curse than a blessing. Midas wished for everything he touched to turn to gold. It did, but he couldn't eat or drink. In some versions of the story he turns his daughter into a golden statue.

- **The Monkey's Paw wish**: In this example, the character wishes for something modest and realistic but it costs them dearly. In W. W. Jacobs' supernatural short story 'The Monkey's Paw', Mr White wishes for just £200. He gets the money but in the form of compensation for the death of his son.

- **Idiot genie wishes**: In this kind of story, the genie grants a wish but not quite how the wisher expected. A wisher might ask to be taller than they are now and be turned into a giraffe. They might ask for eternal youth and be turned into a statue. The genie (or whatever) who grants the wish can be evil or just not very clever.

- **The long way round wish**: These are hard to write but probably the most satisfying stories. A character's wish doesn't seem to be granted properly. Maybe they wished to be fabulously wealthy but ended up homeless and penniless. Through this, they realise the value of what they originally had.

Modern wish stories are often morality tales like the long way round wish: the person who makes the wish just needs to realise that they already have everything they need to be happy.

WHAT DOES YOUR CHARACTER WANT?

> [Successful characters] have a drive to do something – they want to gain something, they want to be rid of something, they want to love a person or find a widget.
>
> Chuck Wendig, *Damn Fine Story*

You have to decide what your main character wants before they make the wish, and their life before they make the wish must reflect this. For example, your main character might be a girl who is lonely – her family are too busy to pay attention to her and she has no friends at school. All she wants is a friend. She gets allocated a new kid who turns out to be the most annoying child in the school. By making the new kid popular, she wins friends herself.

WHAT GRANTS THE WISHES?

You have a number of options here. Take a look at the following:

- It could be a genie. You then have an extra character in the story, which can be fun or can be a distraction. Genies can be evil, sympathetic, sad or dangerous. They can also be woefully out of touch with the modern world after being trapped in a lamp or an old teapot for hundreds of years!

- It could be an object – and it might be cursed. This is entertaining because the object could be an antique, like an old ring, or it could be modern, like a phone. *The Queen's Nose* by Dick King-Smith featured a fifty pence coin that granted wishes. Is the object a gift? Is it discovered?

- It could be fate – in the form of a sudden lottery win or discovery. You might be familiar with Frank Cottrell-Boyce's *Millions*, which uses this trick. Even better, the money will become worthless if they don't spend it quickly.

- It could be a friend whose power and positivity convince our main character that they can have what they want – a character who removes a barrier and allows them to flourish.

- It could be the main character. Sometimes, a meek character decides to do one brave thing and effectively grants themselves the thing they've always wished for by finally taking action. This action might be the result of an event – something that happens to someone else. If the event is positive, our main character might think, 'I want that too.' If it's horrible, negative or fear inducing, it might be the spur our main character needed – the thing that finally changes them.

SMALL FOCUS

When you write a wish story there is a risk that your focus can grow too wide. As tempting as it is, try to wish for small things and keep the spotlight on relationships and family. You might wish to be the greatest footballer in the world, but a running account of your world travels and every match you play will leave your reader cold. Gloss over them and think about how it might affect your friendships. Would other people be jealous?

CHAIN OF WISHES

There have been some excellent stories written about the mess characters make when they try to correct their last wish – making things ten times worse instead. If you have a great idea for this, go for it. Otherwise, steer clear of this sort of complexity: you'll tie your story in knots and end up with a headache.

POSSIBLE ENDINGS

There are two possible endings that are satisfying to the reader:

1. **Back to normal**: The character has learned a lesson, managed to undo all the bad consequences of their wishes and got home in time for tea, a slightly different person as a result of their experiences.

2. **Life will never be the same**: The character has learned a lesson but can never go back to how it was before the wish. Their world has changed irrevocably. They are usually sorry about this.

Of course, you might have another idea!

Once you've decided what your character wants and what will grant them their wish, you're ready to write a scene.

> You can either write from the perspective of the main character or from the third person, outside the character. You're going to add a second character – the wish-giver. They are going to grant the first of three wishes ...
>
> Aim for 300 words. Keep the scene enclosed, using one single location. Cover only a small amount of time. You're going to describe a conversation that takes only a short amount of time, but gets to the heart of your central character's wants.

ACTIVITY 12. WANTS VS. NEEDS

Unreliable narrator (noun): a narrator who isn't credible or believable because they are hiding something from themselves or the reader.

If you want to try something more ambitious, you might consider thinking about your character's wants as well as their needs. There's a difference:

NEEDS

The reader sees these but the character doesn't know about them yet.

'He needs to grow up!'

'She needs to ask her friends for help and stop trying to do it all alone.'

'He needs to have confidence in himself.'

WANTS

The character knows they have these.

'I want to be popular!'

'I want to win the talent competition.'

'I want to find my missing brother.'

The wants are going to be in the foreground of your story – obvious to everyone. The character *knows* they want whatever it is and they talk or think about it. They make plans to get it and the other characters know about it too. The wants form the plot of the story – things start to happen because of these wants.

The needs are going to be in the background. Because the main character *doesn't know* they need to do or be this thing, they don't talk about it or mention it at all. The reader has their opinions though. Other characters might have their opinions too. Needs form the theme of the story, and the character often learns about their needs by the end.

Here are two examples to consider:

1. *Star Wars*: Luke Skywalker *wants* to leave his unremarkable planet and travel the universe. He knows this and complains to his aunt and uncle about it. As viewers, we see that he *needs* to toughen up and start taking responsibility for his life.

2. *Brooklyn Nine-Nine*: Jake Peralta *wants* to impress his boss and be regarded as the best detective in the team. He's driven by this competitive streak and often makes bad decisions as a result. As viewers, we know he *needs* to grow up and be more professional.

Why not try combining these together in unusual or interesting ways? Pick one from each column below and see what story might suggest itself.

Possible character wants	Possible character needs
To find their missing brother/sister.	To be honest and stop telling stories.
To escape from a suffocating, strict boarding school.	To ask for help from others.
To win a tournament or game at all costs.	To forgive themselves for a previous mistake.
To ask someone out on a date.	To learn to trust others.
To defeat or humiliate a villain who has made their life miserable.	To let go of grief and move on.
To recover a lost item.	To be confident.
To get a place at a prestigious summer camp which requires a tough application process.	To trust themselves.

Possible character wants	Possible character needs
To succeed in exams without having to do any work.	To stand up for what they believe in.
To fix a problem they created when they were a foolish kid.	To stop blaming others and see that something is their responsibility.
To cover up a lie they have told – even though it's spinning out of control.	To be brave and take the next step.
To get a seat at a particular table for the end-of-year prom.	To be themselves and stop pretending to be someone else.
To solve a murder.	To admit they have feelings for someone.

Now that you've got a quick summary of what your main character wants and what they actually need, you're ready to write a scene.

You can either write from the perspective of the main character or from the third person, outside the character. You're going to add a second character – a character who can see that the main character has an actual need. The second character is going to try to convince the first to see this need. But your main character isn't ready to admit it. They're just focused on their wants.

Aim for 300 words. Keep the scene enclosed, using one single location. Cover only a small amount of time. You're going to describe a conversation – perhaps an argument – that takes only a short amount of time.

ACTIVITY 13. MISTAKEN WANTS AND THE MOMENT OF REALISATION

Epiphany (noun): a moment of sudden learning or realisation.

John Yorke, in his book *Into the Woods*, suggests that characters are walking contradictions.[2] Here are some examples:

- In Disney's *Tangled*, Flynn Rider is a carefree thief who ends up dedicated to protecting the life of a princess.

- In *Moana*, the central character is desperate to leave her island home and the responsibilities that come with it, but she ends up accepting those responsibilities and leading her tribe.

- In *The Walking Dead*, Morgan Jones has sworn off violence and vows never to kill, but when Carol's life is threatened he becomes her violent protector.

- In *Star Wars*, Han Solo is a cynical smuggler only on the lookout for himself and yet he gets involved in the rebellion and turns out to be a hero.

In the case of Han Solo, he thinks he wants to be wealthy, but actually he wants something more – a cause, something noble to strive for. In the end he becomes a hero. He changes, but more importantly what he thought he wanted wasn't his real goal.

Characters lie to themselves in fiction. Creating a character who thinks they want one thing but ends up with what they really want is challenging. If you can imply it, you'll give your writing greater depth. If you can create a scene in which the character realises they've been mistaken, that's even better.

Professor Steven Reiss, a psychologist at Ohio State University, conducted studies with over 6,000 people to try to define their underlying motivations.[3] Here

---

2   John Yorke, *Into the Woods: How Stories Work and Why We Tell Them* (London: Penguin, 2013), pp. 132–134.

3   Steven Reiss, *Who Am I? The 16 Basic Desires That Motivate Our Actions and Define Our Personalities* (New York: J.P. Tarcher/Putnam, 2000).

are seven motives that we've found useful to consider when we create complex characters:

1. Acceptance: the need for approval, support and good feeling from those around you.

2. Competition: the need to pit yourself against others, to compete and win.

3. Family: the need to raise or help children, to nurture others, to work in small loyal units supporting those around you.

4. Independence: the need for individuality, the ability to organise and run things your way.

5. Power: the need for influence, the ability to determine the direction of others, the responsibility for the performance of groups.

6. Social contact: the need for friends, to have extensive peer relationships.

7. Social status: the need to appear to be of a high social standing or a person of importance.

Imagine a character who wants two of these things, but has them the wrong way round. We have a 'mistaken want' (it might be competition in a character who thinks they need to win at all costs) and a 'real want' (this character might realise they are seeking acceptance from their parents). Consider the options and make a note of the ideas that develop as a result.

Now consider the following grid. It gives you six other ideas to play with:

Number	Mistaken want	Number	Real want
1	Money	1	Friendship
2	A prize	2	Acceptance
3	Admiration	3	Humility
4	Fame	4	Family

Number	Mistaken want	Number	Real want
5	A top job	5	Trust
6	A pet	6	Intimacy or closeness

Once you've got a clear idea of your character's mistaken want, you're ready to write a scene.

You can either write from the perspective of the main character or from the third person, outside the character. Your main character is going to realise they have been pursuing the wrong want. Instead, they suddenly see what it is they really want.

You may need a second character – someone who is shocked by the change they see in the person they thought they knew.

Aim for 300 words. Keep the scene enclosed, using one single location. Cover only a small amount of time. You're going to describe a revelation, a moment of sudden understanding, perhaps a conversation that may last only a short amount of time – but it will have big consequences.

ACTIVITY 14. CREATING CONFLICT

Conflict (noun): a serious disagreement or argument.

Have you ever seen a fight or an argument in the school yard and felt yourself drawn to it? Why do we so love gossip? Whenever there's an argument and we aren't involved, we like nothing better than to get a tub of popcorn, pull up a stool and settle down to watch the chaos that unfolds. We are drawn to conflict.

Conflict can be a full-blown battle between two armies, it could be a fight between two groups of people or it could be an argument between two individuals. Notice the word 'between'. That's where the reader sits, watching, between the two sides.

Have you ever watched a cartoon in which the main character is faced with a dilemma and an angel appears on one shoulder and a devil on the other, each giving advice about what to do next? That's internal conflict: the argument inside the character's head as she decides. Think of Macbeth as he anguishes over whether or not to kill King Duncan. He runs through all the arguments for and against the terrible deed, and the audience are hooked on every word – they want to know what Macbeth will do.

Conflict is the lifeblood of stories. Without it, they die.

Consider this short, two-sentence story:

> One day, I found a £10 note. It wasn't mine, so I handed it in.

We could criticise it for lack of description or the way it fails to use any interesting language, but its main flaw is that it is not interesting to the reader. Any amount of flowery language could not save this story because it lacks conflict or the potential for conflict. If we made it difficult for the protagonist to get the £10 note – to have it blowing away in the wind, for example – we would still be introducing conflict.

Now consider this short, two-sentence story:

> One day, I found a £10 note. It wasn't mine, but, glancing around to see nobody was looking, I slipped it into my pocket.

This has conflict built in. The narrator has stolen the money. He or she is now in conflict with the original owner.

Suddenly the story has potential. The reader is left wondering what he or she would have done in that situation and what will happen next. There are clues about how the next piece of the adventure will fall into place. Maybe someone was watching her. The narrator also has a secret, and secrets are brilliant in stories because someone can betray that secret.

Conflict is what stops our heroine from achieving her goal straight away. Conflict is the supervillain fighting the superhero, or the teacher keeping the main character in detention. Conflict could be a storm at sea, an avalanche or a guilty feeling. The barriers that we put in the way to stop our heroine getting what she wants are conflict.

In this activity, we are asking you to consider where the conflict in your story might come from.

- Is it external – from outside our main character?
- Or is the conflict inside our main character?
- Is the conflict obvious, violent or aggressive?
- Or is it subtle, persuasive and devious?

Have a look at our examples:

External — **from the outside**

A devious friend pretends to be nice to stop your main character

An evil, bloodthirsty vampire tries to stop your main character

Hidden, **subtle**

Obvious, **aggressive**

Your character has an illness they don't yet know about – but you hint at in the story

A terrifying bad dream haunts your character, forcing them to stop pursuing their goal

Internal — **from the character**

The top-right quadrant is an obvious place to start: this is where the classic baddies from stories live. Monsters, evil villains, strict teachers, cruel parents and Darth Vader all belong up here.

But what about the other quadrants? Make a list of as many ideas as you can and place them somewhere on the matrix. Then choose your favourite.

Once you've figured out the source of your conflict, you're ready to write a scene.

> Write a scene in which conflict is introduced between two characters or inside one. It can be from any of the sources you've thought about. It can be from any quadrant of the matrix above.
>
> Conflict creates emotion, so pay attention to how the conflict is affecting your characters.
>
> Conflict is often expressed through dialogue, so make sure your characters are expressing their differences and disagreements.
>
> Aim for 300 words. Keep your scene enclosed, using a single location.

ACTIVITY 15. CHARACTER TICS

Tic (noun): a nervous twitch or frequently repeated action.

Most people have some kind of mannerism – something they say or do with such frequency that it's what you remember about them once they've gone. Sometimes, giving a supporting character a tic is a great way of making them seem less two-dimensional.

It may be a 'catchphrase'. Jon's uncle couldn't help but pepper his sentences with the phrase 'you know, like'. He would tell you about a holiday and say, 'The sun came out every, you know, like, day.' Or, 'We had these, you know, like, deck-chairs on the beach, like.' Obviously, the writer has to be careful not to overdo this, but a couple of catchphrases carefully inserted into dialogue can bring a character to life.

A club bouncer may seem like a cardboard cut-out gorilla, until you give him or her a strange habit of always humming a certain tune or constantly clearing their throat. Suddenly, they're mildly interesting. It doesn't have to go any further than that.

Similarly, a physical tic can be interesting too. It doesn't have to be an actual twitch, although that is an option. Characters could fiddle with a favourite object – twirling a coin around their fingers, for example. They may be a nail biter, a hair twirler or a foot tapper. These tics might hint at their wants or needs. Perhaps they might highlight their anxieties or fears.

Another word of caution: restrict character tics to one supporting character, two at the most, otherwise the cast of the book will be nail biting, hair twirling and head scratching all the time and it will distract the reader from the events of the story.

COLLECTING TICS

Make a list of the physical mannerisms of people you know, or if you want to randomise the process pick the month of your birth and use the mannerism from the following table.

Month	Mannerism	Month	Mannerism
January	Nail biting	July	Weird stretching
February	Hair twirling	August	Yawning
March	Knuckle cracking	September	Ear pulling
April	Nose scratching	October	Nail picking
May	Long slow blinking	November	Cuff straightening
June	Head scratching	December	Jewellery adjustment

CATCHPHRASES

Again, make a list of verbal tics or catchphrases that a character could use. They may occur frequently in a character's dialogue, rather like Jon's uncle, or they could be used a little less. A good example of this might be a teacher who says, 'I won't tell you again' or a waiter who asks, 'Is everything all right?' a little too often.

COHERENCE

Combining a physical and verbal tic is a great thing to do. To maximise the effect both tics should be coherent – that is, they should make sense together. A good example of this might be a character who is always making sure there is no dirt on their hands or clothes and who is also sloppy about their speech. The two tics don't go together. It is much better if that character speaks precisely – it supports the images of neat and rule-following fastidiousness. A character who is nervous might apologise a lot and adjust their cuffs constantly.

DISSONANCE

Just to complicate matters, sometimes it can be fun to have a character who has tics that seem to contradict their position – the apologetic hitman or the aggressive elf at Santa's grotto.

Once you've listed a range of physical and verbal tics, you're ready to write a scene.

Write a piece of dialogue between two characters with different positions and intentions. You could start by considering a teacher and a parent at parents' evening – let's imagine the child hasn't done very well this term and the parent is defending them.

Or select two different characters. Whoever you choose, make sure there is conflict.

Give one of the characters a tic. Remember not to overload the narrative – mention it two or three times only.

Aim for 300 words. Keep your scene enclosed, using a single location.

ACTIVITY 16. A DOZEN LUCKY CHARMS

Talisman (noun): an object thought to have significant power or importance.

Often, all it takes is for a character to have one object of importance on them at all times, and suddenly they rise above the ordinary. The act of treasuring something indirectly creates a set of implied attitudes, values and concerns that begin to filter into the storytelling. A little like a character tic, a lucky charm or talisman makes a character seem more real.

If forced to come up with a list of lucky charms on the spot, we might find ourselves thinking of clichés: a horseshoe hanging on the door of a house, a four-leaf clover or a lucky number. Even a rabbit's foot, cut off the animal and carried on a key ring, is apparently considered lucky. We need to steer clear of these in stories if we're going to surprise and interest our readers.

In this activity, you have to spend some time thinking about a character who has an unusual charm or talisman. They might carry it with them regularly, and they might hold it or cradle it when times are tough or when they need to make an important decision.

Your aim is to take a potentially ordinary object and give it new meaning, significance or power by making it into a special lucky charm. Your character will come alive as you think about what their talisman is and why they treasure it.

Use the following diagram to get you thinking. Aim to generate a dozen possible ideas.

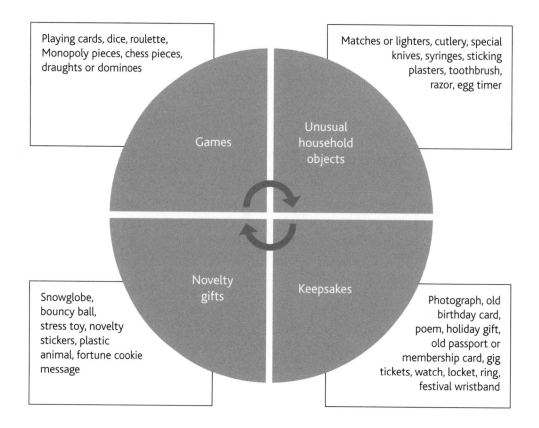

Playing cards, dice, roulette, Monopoly pieces, chess pieces, draughts or dominoes

Matches or lighters, cutlery, special knives, syringes, sticking plasters, toothbrush, razor, egg timer

Games

Unusual household objects

Novelty gifts

Keepsakes

Snowglobe, bouncy ball, stress toy, novelty stickers, plastic animal, fortune cookie message

Photograph, old birthday card, poem, holiday gift, old passport or membership card, gig tickets, watch, locket, ring, festival wristband

Once you've generated your ideas and decided on your favourite, sketch out a brief summary of your character and their talisman – outline the significance/meaning in a few sentences.

You might want to use the following as an example:

> Character A puts fresh sticking plasters on his knuckles at the start of each day, then draws letters on them in biro – one letter per plaster. His father, now in prison, had letters tattooed on the backs of his fingers – LOVE and HATE. Character A has strong, fond memories of his dad, but at the same time he doesn't want to end up like him, so their daily messages are different.

Once you've got a quick summary, you're ready to write a scene in which you introduce the character using their talisman in an unusual way. Write from the

ACTIVITY 16

perspective of someone who doesn't know the character well and is witnessing this strange behaviour for the first time.

> Aim for 300 words. Keep the scene enclosed, using one single location. Cover only a small amount of time. You're going to describe something that takes two or three minutes to happen, with the talisman being used in some way. Try to capture the watching character's surprise at seeing the talisman used for the first time.

ACTIVITY 17. THE SWAPPED COAT

Have you ever picked up something that didn't belong to you by accident? Something that looks similar to something you own but turns out to belong to someone else? A stranger, perhaps, or someone with a secret.

In this activity, you will begin a story with one character investigating the pockets of someone else's coat. Get ready by deciding if your character might have:

- Picked up the coat thinking it belongs to them and be entirely innocent.

- Deliberately stolen the coat for a reason you need to decide.

- Found an opportunity to search the pockets very quickly for a reason you need to decide.

WHAT'S IN THOSE POCKETS?

There can be either one or two items in the pockets, that's up to you. You can choose anything at all, but since restricting choice boosts creativity, we've suggested twenty-six possibilities, one for each letter of the alphabet.

Choose your two favourite objects. Or if you want random objects, choose the two objects associated with the first two letters of your name or your initials.

Letter	Item	Letter	Item
A	A filled out form for a lottery ticket.	N	A map of Manchester with a scribbled 'X'.
B	A card with the message 'Winners never quit'.	O	A pack of playing cards with the hearts suit missing.
C	A bottle of pills. The text is in Spanish.	P	A silver lighter inscribed 'For C'.

ACTIVITY 17

Letter	Item	Letter	Item
D	A metal hipflask with some liquid in it.	Q	A single bullet.
E	The keys to a vintage BMW.	R	A diary with every page after 5th November torn out.
F	A Fitbit with a snapped strap.	S	A passport photo ripped into fifteen pieces.
G	A receipt for a long taxi journey: £200.	T	A phone – no call history but one contact.
H	A newspaper article about an airplane crash.	U	A folded A4 poster for a lost dog called Eagle.
I	A library book checked out in Edinburgh.	V	A watch like the one nurses pin to their uniform.
J	A letter – a hospital appointment for tomorrow.	W	A small blue speckled egg.
K	A wedding ring with a faded inscription.	X	A timetable showing high and low tide.
L	A handful of coins – two of them are Russian.	Y	A library card with an unreadable signature.
M	Fingernails – loads of them.	Z	A document wallet full of weather forecasts.

How does your character feel as they discover these objects? Confused, for sure, but what after that? What might the objects signify? Who might they belong to? And why are they important to your character?

Once you've thought it through and chosen your objects, you're ready to write a scene.

> Aim for 400 words, exploring the discovery of these items. Switch between descriptions of the items, the emotional response of your main character and tension about discovery. Keep the scene enclosed, using one single location. Cover only a small amount of time. You're going to describe something that takes two or three minutes to happen.
>
> Close the scene with another character entering and noticing what's been taking place.

ACTIVITY 18. LOST AND FOUND

Once you establish that a character has an important talisman or lucky charm, you can inject drama by having that item go missing.

Imagine a character whose life revolves around a particularly important object. Look back at the notes and ideas you have so far about talismans to help you choose one.

There are two ways to approach this activity. One is to focus on loss and the other is to describe an unexpected find. Reflect on these options in a little more detail before you make your choice.

OPTION 1:

Consider what it might be like for a person to discover that their most important object is unexpectedly missing. Think about where they might have lost it before you begin. Which of these would be most dramatic here?

- A private, domestic setting – the character searches drawers and wardrobes.
- A public setting – the character searches the floor of a busy train station with people milling about, announcements coming over the tannoy and a busker playing a violin.

OPTION 2:

Consider what it might be like if a character lost an important item many years ago – a talisman that meant a lot to them when they were much younger. Now have them rediscover it. They're not expecting to find it and it comes as a shock! Before you begin, think about the setting. Which of these might be more dramatic?

- A safe, domestic setting, with a character alone searching their old bedroom.
- An unexpected public setting – the character sees the object in the pool of a public fountain. At first they can't believe their eyes …

Once you've made a decision, you're ready to write.

> Aim for 400 words. Switch between a description of the item and the emotional response of your main character. How does your character feel as they realise they have lost their talisman? Or rediscovered a significant object?
>
> Keep the scene enclosed, using one single location. Cover only a small amount of time. You're going to describe something that takes two or three minutes to happen.

ACTIVITY 19. FLAW AND CHALLENGE

Hamartia (noun): a fatal flaw that leads to a character's downfall.

Someone's Achilles heel is their weak spot: a character flaw that makes them less than invincible. All of us are imperfect, but often when we write stories our imaginations reach for the characters we're used to from children's stories.

Back in the days when we were read fairy tales at school or at bedtime, we all became used to two-dimensional characters – 'goodies' and 'baddies'. The goodies were perfect, strong and dedicated. The baddies were evil, selfish and despicable. But in more complex stories characters are flawed; as a result they become more interesting.

Here's an example: which hero is more interesting, Superman or Batman? Not your favourite, just the most interesting. Debate is usually split for a while, but Batman usually comes out as the most interesting. Why? Perhaps Superman's just a little too perfect.

In this activity, you're going to create characters with Achilles heels, with flaws. You'll be surprised to discover that once you're writing a flawed character, better plot ideas emerge.

Take the following examples. On the left is a character flaw. On the right is space for you to come up with a challenge that the character might have to face. An interesting story often emerges if you place a flawed character in an uncomfortable position. Have a go!

Flaw	Challenge they could face
A fear of heights.	
A belief that they're cleverer than anyone else.	

Flaw	Challenge they could face
An obsession with how they appear on social media.	
A greed for money.	
Lack of leadership qualities and belief in themselves.	
Makes bad decisions under pressure.	
Claustrophobia.	

Each one of these character flaws might suggest a scenario in which they are challenged and experience great discomfort before overcoming their fears or weaknesses. Which one suggested the most interesting scenario to you?

Once you've chosen, you're ready to write.

Aim for 400 words in total. Begin in the middle of things (*in medias res*), throwing your character into a difficult situation.

Focus on the internal emotion – the physical symptoms of stress or terror, for example – but don't forget to balance your piece with descriptions of place and character.

Of course, keep the scene enclosed, using your single chosen location. Cover only a small amount of time.

Consider closing the scene with an action, taken reluctantly and in fear by your main character – a moment of great courage as they begin to face their fear.

ACTIVITY 19

ACTIVITY 20. JOINING THE DARK SIDE: GIVING YOUR CHARACTER AN EDGE

Moral ambiguity (noun): a lack of consistent moral clarity in decision-making and behaviour.

We all like to think of ourselves as good people. Research by psychologists from Goldsmiths, University of London suggests that, ridiculously, 98% of British people think they're within the nicest 50% of the population.[4]

We pride ourselves on giving to charity and helping people. Being kind to others who are less fortunate is considered a virtue. As a result of this, generally speaking, our public persona – the person we like other people to think we are – is agreeable and polite, maybe even helpful and cooperative. We display to others the virtues that are promoted by the society in which we live. Schools are a great example of this. Think about how the vast majority of students speak to teachers compared with how they might address each other. Then consider how the thoughts in our heads contrast with the words from our lips.

Our instinct is to be agreeable, helpful, kind and considerate when we are on public display. The trouble is that writing in school is a very public activity. A teacher or a peer might be reviewing your work, and so your guard is up when you bring your character to life on the page. This means your character is either going to be insufferably reasonable or a victim. These characters lack agency: instead of *doing things*, things are *done to them*.

One way to remedy this is to think about your less appealing or 'secret' side. This is difficult to do because we're all hardwired to be agreeable. We don't want other people to see our bad side.

At this point it is important to realise something else: if you are writing about a character, that character is not a real person, even if you are writing about yourself when you were eight. It is a work of fiction. You may try to make that character realistic and you may try to portray your emotions as accurately as you can remember them, but it is still not 100% true. Writers of historical fiction

---

4   Simon Usborne, 'Why Do We Think We're Nicer Than We Actually Are?', *The Guardian* (13 March 2017). Available at: https://www.theguardian.com/science/shortcuts/2017/mar/13/why-do-we-think-were-nicer-than-we-actually-are.

can only use their imaginations to recreate the past, even if they do meticulous research, and the same is true when trying to capture a memory or an event. The person in the story is *not* you. Keep this in mind.

For a moment, consider some of your less appealing habits or impulses. What would your character be like if they picked their nose? How would you react to a character if they were a bully or a thief?

FRAMING THE CHARACTER

Put simply, when writing about a childhood memory, is there any way you can make the main character into a villain? Rather than being pushed off a climbing frame as a child, could your main character be the one doing the pushing? What are the motives? What are the consequences? Could your main character be caught shoplifting?

NEGATIVE EMOTIONS

A student remembers that he once dropped a chunk of chocolate and his grandmother's dog ate it, making it sick. He felt guilty and awful. This makes an interesting anecdote, but if we give the main character a few negative emotions towards the dog then the story comes alive.

What if he had done it on purpose? What if he hated that dog? Perhaps it yapped constantly when he was trying to talk to his grandmother or terrified him when he was young. Maybe it bit him.

IMPULSE VILLAINS – THE POWER OF BAD DECISIONS

Impulse villainy is great for starting a story off. The things that a character does without thinking always lead to trouble, precisely because the character hasn't thought where their actions might lead.

What would you do if you found a £20 note on the floor? Keep it? (Interesting!) Hand it in? (Dull.)

What if you kept it but then found someone in the class in tears because they had lost their money for the trip to a local theme park? You have the money in your pocket. You have the power to end their misery. Do you? Or is there some reason for you to keep that money?

Making the wrong decision always leads to an interesting story because one bad turn should always lead to another, making the narrative more complex and interesting. Once the main character is in the wrong, they are open to blackmail, telling lies and committing more crimes.

THE BEST VILLAINS THINK THEY ARE A HERO

Of course, the danger is that the character created in this way becomes a pantomime villain, laughing gleefully at their evil deeds. It is better to have a nuanced villain.

Remember the research which suggests that 98% of people think they are the nicest people in the country? Some of those people have just got to be villains in someone else's story. Maybe they're a mean boss or a sarcastic teacher. None of us are perfect all the time, and none of us are awfully behaved all the time.

Maybe your character can be a mix too: 'I'm keeping the £20 note because my mum just lost her job and I daren't ask for any more money.' Instantly, we have a chance to feel sorry for the character even though they've done something bad. It sets up a dilemma in our own heads: are we on the main character's side or against them?

Once you've considered these options and made some decisions, you're ready to write a scene.

> You're going to write from the perspective of a character with an edge – a dark side. You don't have to make them a monster; perhaps they'll be more interesting and creepy if they appear to be in some ways normal.
>
> You're going to tell a brief story. By the end, the reader will have recognised their darker side too.
>
> Aim for 300 words. Limit your story to a single scene. Keep it enclosed, using a single chosen location. Cover only a small amount of time.

CHAPTER 4

CRAFTING SETTINGS

PLACE AND PERSON: SEARCHING FOR CONTRASTS

In the early stages of creative practice, the imagination replicates rather than innovates. There's nothing wrong with that, it's an important stage in the process. But we can push students towards innovation more quickly by seeking out contrast rather than complement.

This can be applied to place and person. Many exam questions provide a place – usually via the medium of a picture – and students respond on the day of the exam by populating it with characters. When a student replicates they draw on memories of experiences or texts and populate their setting with stock characters, all of whom have a good reason to be there.

Here are a few examples:

- A picture of a beach is provided. Drawing on stock texts or personal experiences, the student replicates. They choose a cast of characters that include: a family on holiday, an ice cream shack and a lifeguard.

- The task is to set a story in an abandoned house. Stock replication gives you a limited range of options. The student chooses: a man whose car has broken down seeking help, a mysterious butler or evil crone, or perhaps a group of students challenging themselves to sleep overnight.

- A picture of snow-capped peaks produces: a mountaineer, two friends on holiday and a helicopter pilot.

A fresh approach might be to actively seek out contrasts. Characters or objects that seem immediately out of place feel fresh, unusual and different.

Of course, locations also lend coherence, mood and atmosphere to a piece. It's surprising how many student narratives don't exploit the power of the weather. Its metaphorical significance can create colour, mood and a coherence of imagery and feel which can contribute to a sense of shape and structure. The same goes for extended metaphors and patterns of imagery. This all requires observation and sensual writing.

This chapter will suggest a number of activities to help your students combine character and location in a more innovative way.

ACTIVITY 21. INSTANT PATHETIC FALLACY

Pathetic fallacy (noun): the use of inanimate things such as the weather to mirror human moods or emotions.

CREATING MOOD IN YOUR WRITING: USING THE WEATHER!

If there is a funeral in a film, the weather will almost always be rainy and dull. It shows the mood of the characters through the weather. This is called the pathetic fallacy and it is a great technique to use.

Craft a sentence to describe a storm by picking a word from each column below. For example: 'Angry clouds screamed across the skies.'

Mood	Subject	Verb	Object
Angry, furious, irate, vexed, irritated, exasperated, indignant, aggrieved, galled, resentful, wrathful, vengeful	Clouds, rain, lightning, thunder, wind, hailstones, snow	Lashed, beat, whipped, slapped, flailed, punched, howled, screamed, clawed, shook, lacerated, stabbed	Trees, forest, woods, hills, valley, plains, rooftops, houses, streets, cars, skies

You can expand the sentence using colour or some other adjectives or even a simile or metaphor. Then make two more sentences.

Repeat the exercise using the following table. Discuss why these sentences feel different to the first ones.

Mood	Subject	Verb	Object
Sly, crafty, sullen, unhappy, cruel, mean, threatening, hungry	Fog, mist, darkness, shadows, twilight, night, half-light	Crept, slithered, sneaked, slid, smothered, wormed, inched, edged, lurked, skulked	Trees, forest, woods, hills, valley, plains, rooftops, houses, streets, cars, skies

Mood words are great when they are used to describe an object: 'sullen clouds', 'irritated cars' or 'threatening trees'. They give your objects a life of their own. They don't have to be angry or threatening: a 'cheerful armchair' sounds like just the kind of thing you'd want to sit in, for example.

Now consider what mood you would like a story or scene to have. You're going to conjure up that mood through the weather.

Once you've decided on your mood and atmosphere, you're ready to write. Your aim is going to be 300 words.

Present your reader with a moody, vivid description of a character in a place. Make sure your character is doing something, even if it's just walking, and use the weather to help create a strong sense of mood and atmosphere.

Consider playing with light and dark, day and night, sound and colour as well as the weather.

Focus about 50% of your writing on the location and weather, and the other 50% on your central character and what they're doing. Consider a contrast between the location, the mood and the actions of the character.

Focus on a single chosen location and cover only a small amount of time.

ACTIVITY 22. WELCOME TO THE JUNGLE: EXTENDED METAPHORS

Extended metaphor (noun): a metaphor that is repeated or used at length in adjusted form throughout a story.

The mood of your setting may be determined by your use of the pathetic fallacy (discussed in Activity 21), but you will need more than that to create a mood that seeps through your entire work.

Extended metaphors will bind your story together and give it a unity that will please the reader.

To achieve this, the author has to first decide whether their setting is populated or unpopulated. By this we mean, quite simply, does your setting have more than one or two people in it?

If it has more than one person in it, then it is populated and you can use the people as part of the scenery.

POPULATED

Think of your setting. You might want to choose one of the following:

- A beach busy with sunbathers and a distant storm at sea.
- A busy shopping centre, perhaps with a character searching for a lost item.
- A school canteen at breaktime.
- A bright and vibrant wedding with hundreds of guests and a string quartet playing classical music.

Once you've decided, you have to try to describe one setting using the language from another. Take the final example of a wedding: you may choose to describe the guests in terms that would suggest another setting, like a circus or a zoo.

Some people at the wedding will be clowns, messing up the bride and groom's car before they leave and playing practical jokes. Another person, the best man, might be the ringmaster trying to keep order. Others will be the audience, looking on with different levels of disapproval. Some people might dance like acrobats, others might clap like seals. You get the idea.

UNPOPULATED

If you're choosing an unpopulated location, you don't have the luxury – or challenge – of describing people. You might be considering:

- A snow-choked forest.
- The windswept shoulder of a mountain.
- A Pacific island of deep jungle with an abandoned clearing.
- An empty multi-storey car park at midnight.
- The interior of a broken-down barn isolated in a huge field of corn.

Without characters to focus on in your unpopulated setting, it might be useful to pick a type of animal and use it to describe the weather or a particular aspect of the landscape.

A storm could be a raging bull tossing leaves and umbrellas on its horns, bellowing with rage and knocking over bins. Laundry on a line could be like a matador's cloak. Branches snapped from trees could be his lance or the bull's horns.

MASH IT UP

Of course, just to confuse matters, some unpopulated settings lend themselves to a populated approach. Think of a garden full of exotic plants and flowers; this could easily be described in terms of a zoo or a circus. Each plant would take on the characteristics of an animal or a performer. In this case, the plants are the characters – they are like people.

Once you've made some decisions about your setting – such as whether it will be a populated or unpopulated location – and you've chosen an extended metaphor, you're ready to write.

> Aim for around 300 words. Describe one of the settings provided in the left-hand column of the table below in terms of another setting provided in the right-hand column, or describe one setting using an extended metaphor.

Setting 1	Setting 2
A wedding	A zoo
A shopping centre	A circus
A festival	A battle
A stormy beach	A wrestling match
A deserted, out-of-season ski resort	A carnival parade

> Place a character in your location. Make sure your character is doing something, even if it's just walking, and use the weather to help create a strong sense of mood and atmosphere.
>
> Focus on a single chosen location but cover as much time as you want.

ACTIVITY 23. MAKING THE SENSES WORK FOR YOU

Personification (noun): the attribution of human characteristics to something non-human.

One piece of advice frequently given to students of writing is to describe things using all the senses. This is good advice, but it has become something of a cliché and therefore lost some of its meaning. Of course we write what we see or hear – perception is our only gateway to these experiences – so why wouldn't we write using the senses?

If we tell you to write describing what you sense then it becomes a little clearer – for example, 'I could smell toffee apples mingled with sooty diesel fumes.'

Yes, you are looking for a description that will create a scene in the reader's head, but this is a bit of a dull sensory checklist. It also feels unrealistic: nobody ever stands in one place checking off what they can see, hear, taste and smell. Not unless they are spies or undercover police officers.

If we ask, what were the smells *doing*, that might lead to a more active description: 'The smell of toffee apples mingled with sooty diesel fumes.'

For a really effective piece, we must have a good reason for including the description. How does it affect the main character? What mood does it create? 'The smell of toffee apples mingled with sooty diesel fumes, choking me and making me want to push through the stifling crowd and run away.'

This is tied in with what effect you are trying to create with your writing. If you are intending to create a sense of fear, then smells and sounds are going to be on the attack. Smells might suffocate or force themselves on you. Sounds might crash against your ears or tear through your skull.

If your character is in a good mood, then smells might tickle their nose or maybe even tap them on the shoulder.

Once you've developed some thoughts about the senses, you're ready to write.

You're going to write about food in this scene. You could consider a banquet, a restaurant, a lavish picnic or a meal to mark an important occasion. Or you might want your character to be walking past a chip shop, for example.

Choose the mood your central character is in:

1	Very hungry
2	Feeling sick
3	Angry
4	Bitterly disappointed after a personal setback; sad and isolated
5	Happy, optimistic
6	Exhausted

Now describe the effect the sights, sounds and smells have according to the mood of your character. Aim for 300 words.

Remember to have the senses *doing* things – you're personifying them.

Make sure your character also does something, even if it's just walking along. Give the scene a sense of movement by ensuring that your character is active as well as their senses!

ACTIVITY 24. A HIERARCHY OF SENSES

Hierarchy (noun): a ranking system, often using order of importance.

There's a reason that the audience don't get to see a complete dinosaur until twenty minutes into the original *Jurassic Park* film. You see a poor worker dragged to his death in the opening scene but you don't see the velociraptor until much later. That's because the film-makers want to keep the audience interested.

If you have ever fed a dog, you'll realise that the moment you put the bowl of food on the floor, the dog is no longer interested in you. Its attention has turned to the food. If you hold the food out of reach the dog will look up attentively, waiting for the feast. If you feed the dog by hand one biscuit at a time, you will have its full attention.

Readers are the same.

If you are writing a story, you want your reader to keep on reading. You do this by holding back information or, more accurately, by giving out information one measly crumb at a time. You have their attention. We create questions in the reader's mind. We want to make them curious about what will happen next.

Often in stories you hear something or catch a glimpse of part of it before you see it in full. This is very true of stories that involve the unknown or supernatural forces. Sometimes, a smell might be the first indicator of the presence of something. Then a sound – faint whisperings perhaps. Then the character may notice shadows at the end of a passage. Finally, they will come face-to-face with the terror that is stalking them.

Using this hierarchy of senses is a great way to build tension too.

WHAT WAS THAT NOISE?

Using ideas from the following table, begin thinking about a character who is exploring a space and slowly becomes aware that they are not alone. You should consider spaces that seem empty. If you're stuck you might want to consider:

■ The lower decks of a ship.

- An empty library.
- The top floor of a partially constructed skyscraper.
- The maze-like corridors of an old hotel.
- A ski lodge.

Sense	Just a hint	What was that?	OMG!
Touch/ feeling	A cold breeze. A sense of something moving past you.	A hand on your shoulder. Something barges into you.	Physically attacked by some force. Freezing cold.
Sound	A faint whisper or a sigh. Indistinct. Barely heard. You could be mistaken.	A voice calling your name. Clear. Maybe crying or music in another room.	The ghost speaks. Tells you to get out. Screams.
Sight	A movement in the corner of your eye. A shadow in a window.	A face in the mirror. A glimpsed form dashing from a room. Seeing things that suggest a ghost – for example, things being displaced.	Things might move. You may see the ghost in all its horrific detail. Real evidence that you have encountered a spirit.
Smell	Faint. Nose-tickling. Slightly unpleasant.	Stronger smell might cause the character to wrinkle their nose or cough slightly.	Disgusting, may induce vomiting or total revulsion. Character may need to get away from the noxious stench.

Sense	Just a hint	What was that?	OMG!
Taste (not often used)	Maybe something just doesn't taste right?	Tastes horrible?	Makes you sick, taste blood or bite your tongue. Trying not to scream.
Emotion	Nervous but disbelieving. Dismissing things as nonsense. Explaining them away.	Feelings of fear. Less certain about any explanation. Heart pounding, holding breath. What will happen next?	Total fear. Screaming, frozen to the spot or running away. Heart exploding! Sweating, eyes wide.

Once you've decided on your location and planned out how the hierarchy of senses will work, you're ready to write a scene.

Present your reader with a description of a character moving through a place. Refer back to the sense grid above as you write.

Consider playing with light and dark, day and night, colour and weather to build tension and suspense.

Concentrate about 50% of your writing on the location and the other 50% on your central character and what they're doing and feeling.

Focus on one single chosen location and aim for 300 words.

ACTIVITY 25. PUBLIC VS. PRIVATE

Juxtaposition (noun): a deliberate striking contrast created by putting two opposing things together.

In this activity you're going to consider a vibrant public event, and turn it into something much more strange or sinister by introducing an unexpected character with a private significance for someone present.

Consider a wedding reception, for example. It's a public event: perhaps there's a white marquee with circular tables, silver cutlery and napkins. Maybe there's a place of religious significance and gathered family members dressed in traditional clothing. Perhaps there are musicians or entertainers moving through the crowd. There is certainly laughter and a mood of celebration.

Now consider this: who might arrive to ruin it? And what private motivation might they have?

Next, you could consider a similar public gathering. List all of the elements you would need to create a setting with a strong feeling of positivity, happiness or celebration. Choose one or more of the following to get you thinking:

- An important birthday party.
- A religious ceremony.
- A baby shower.
- A charity dinner event with speeches.
- An awards evening.
- An end-of-year prom or certificate-giving event.

For each of these possibilities, ask yourself, who might arrive to ruin it?

'Ruin' might not mean total chaos. Think of your disturbance on the following scale:

Discomfort, unease, embarrassment   All-out chaos, violence, disaster

The more dramatic option might be something awkward or uncomfortable towards the left-hand side of the scale, but think about whether you can be subtle. A full-scale fight might be challenging to capture!

Once you've made your decision, you're ready to write.

Aim for 400 words in total. Use 200 words to establish the normality of the event. Use your description to capture the positivity and mood of celebration. Introduce and describe some of the characters attending the event.

Now introduce your new character – the person who is going to ruin the proceedings somehow. You've got 200 words to do this. Focus on the shock and tension – the responses of the guests as they realise the atmosphere has changed.

Of course, keep the scene enclosed, using your single chosen location. Cover only a small amount of time. Consider closing the scene with a single line of powerful dialogue spoken by the intruder.

ACTIVITY 26. CHANGING PARAMETERS

Parameter (noun): a limit or boundary which defines the scope, size or shape of something.

Often our imagination generates a safe domestic environment. This makes it harder to add tension or heighten drama. You might be planning a dramatic confrontation but your first thought might be to set it in a canteen, a library or a street corner.

What follows are a series of suggestions for raising the stakes in your setting so that your story suddenly feels edgy and dramatic. Your actual scene doesn't have to change much; you just have to create some new parameters – new height, depth or danger.

HEIGHT

A scene is injected with extra drama if played out at height. Think about:

- A rooftop swimming pool.
- The top floor of a hotel – a room with city views and a balcony.
- A cliff-top path.
- A hot air balloon, airplane, ski lift or bridge.

DEPTH

A scene that occurs underground often benefits from a claustrophobic sense of entrapment. Think about:

- A network of dimly lit cellars.
- An underground bunker.
- A series of flooded caves.
- An underground station or railway tunnel.

LIGHT AND DARK

Often, a scene can benefit from dramatic lighting – a strobing between light and dark adds atmosphere and menace. Think about:

- Torches partially illuminating a dark space.

- The flashing reds and blues of emergency lights – police cars and ambulances.

- The dull red lights that indicate temporary emergency lighting.

- Points of flickering light – campsite fires, forest fires, burning torches or distant lighthouses.

WILDNESS

Characters immediately feel more insecure and insignificant if their location implies a powerful force of nature liable to crush them at any moment. Think about:

- Huge, roaring waterfalls sending up clouds of spray.

- A winter wilderness – frozen rivers, deep snow, leafless trees and wild animals.

- A windswept moorland of single-track roads and dangerous marshland.

- A beach at night, with treacherous rocks and the thundering sea beyond.

Choose one of the parameters above – height, depth, light and dark or wildness. Your task is to use it to form the background to a dramatic scene.

ACTIVITY 26

Once you've chosen, you're ready to write.

Aim for 400 words — and make sure that the location becomes an active part of the story. Break up the scene with reminders of the location so the reader doesn't forget. Make sure the setting makes the scene more dramatic — emphasise danger or atmosphere if you can.

Keep the scene enclosed, using your single chosen location. Cover only a small amount of time. You're going to describe something that takes two or three minutes to happen.

ACTIVITY 27. PEOPLE OUT OF PLACE

When we're trying to build a story on the spot, our imagination often reaches for well-known movies, stories or experiences. We borrow lots of familiar ideas and end up creating something unremarkable – perhaps even a bit boring. Our reader has seen the same sorts of movies and read the same sorts of books that we have and ends up unimpressed.

This often happens with characters and locations. We're given a location to work with and end up filling it with characters, all of whom belong there. It's the way our imaginations work under pressure.

- We're shown a common room and study area and … we put students in it.
- We're given a picture of a forest path and … we place a couple of hikers with backpacks on it.
- We're shown a museum and … we fill it with tourists and families.

What if we could halt this process and instead do something fresh? Our readers would be surprised, and might feel energised and interested. This activity helps you to begin this process.

In the left-hand column of the following table are six places and on the right are twelve characters (thirteen if you count the pair!).

Look at the safe options there – the ones you feel are obvious. Ignore them. Instead select the weirdest and strangest options. They might seem illogical or bizarre, but in a while they might begin to fill you with inspiration and energy!

Places	People
1. A vast stately home with huge gardens, a fountain and a gravel drive.	1. A scientist in a lab coat and safety goggles, with wild hair and a desperate expression.

Places	People
2. A windswept beach with a gathering storm out at sea.	2. Two characters in bathing suits, still wet from the water, shivering and running as if escaping from something.
3. A silent library with high wooden bookcases and neatly arranged reading desks.	3. An explorer – a rough sleeper with a tent in their backpack, mud-caked boots, filthy skin and a shotgun.
4. An indoor swimming pool with steam rooms, a plunge pool and a hot tub, and white plastic recliners with fresh towels.	4. A dinosaur – real, alive, huge and ravenously hungry.
5. The lobby of a grand hotel – glittering chandeliers, plush carpets and gentle classical music.	5. A sophisticated character in evening dress and with immaculate hair, holding a champagne glass and a mobile phone.
6. A wild mountain crag rising above a forest of pines, and a single path climbing up through the mist.	6. A tall character in a long trench coat and heavy black boots. Their face is hidden beneath a wrapped scarf, with only their eyes showing.
	7. A ghost of a character in Victorian dress carrying a silver tray with glasses, a bottle of whisky and two pistols.

Places	People
	8. An academic researcher with piles of ancient books, a pad stuffed with scribbled notes and an unfolded map.
	9. A person in a wedding dress – long, white and lacy – carrying a bouquet of blue flowers.
	10. A police officer, injured at the shoulder, bleeding and walking with a limp, trying to operate a wrecked radio.
	11. A violin player carrying their instrument, playing as they walk.
	12. A person dragging an inflatable dinghy and carrying a paddle over one shoulder.

Once you've decided on your contrasts, you're ready to write.

Aim for 400 words – and convey the strangeness and out-of-place-ness of the character. Keep the scene enclosed, using your single chosen location.

Cover only a small amount of time. You're going to describe something that takes two or three minutes to happen – the arrival of this unusual character.

Close the scene with a line of vivid description or a single line of powerful dialogue.

ACTIVITY 28. OBJECTS OUT OF PLACE

If you've had a go at the previous activities, you'll have seen that stories often come alive when we consider unexpected contradictions rather than reproduce commonly used ideas.

This is another activity that encourages you to explore contrasts – this time by placing an object in an unexpected place. The place will be beautifully clean and precise, and the object will, by contrast, be unexpected, ugly or frightening.

You'll need to describe the scene through the eyes of a character used to the spotlessly perfect scenario. They feel shocked and disturbed by the discovery of the object.

For your setting, either choose one of the two suggested options that follow or generate one of your own.

1. A large and modern detached house screened by trees and a vast garden. Inside, it is plush and immaculately decorated. The kitchen is sleek and modern, mostly white, its surfaces polished to a gleam. The floor is pale marble. It is night. The kitchen is half-dark, lit only by the light from the cooker hood.

2. A private library in a big old house in its own grounds. The floor is polished wood. There is a rug before the fireplace, with two deep leather armchairs and a side table. It is night, and a fire glows in the grate. There is a large heavy desk with a reading lamp. The walls are lined with books.

Your character is going to enter this room. They know the room well and are not expecting to see the object – it wasn't there when they were last in the room. You're going to need to choose the item carefully. This list might help to inspire you:

- A dead bird or other small animal.

- A wheelchair.

- A plumber's workbag, open, with rusty tools lying within.

- A doll.

- Scattered smashed glass and spilled water, as if something has been dropped.

- A pair of mud-encrusted boots.

- The remains of something that has been partially burnt.

- A pair of white silk gloves, damaged or torn in some way or covered in dirt or grime.

- Some sort of weapon.

Once you've decided on your location and object, you're ready to write.

Aim for 400 words – and convey the shock, fear or puzzlement of discovering the unusual object. You might want to consider how you could make the item mean something to the character – perhaps they recognise it.

Keep the scene enclosed, using your single chosen location. Cover only a small amount of time. You're going to describe something that takes two or three minutes to happen.

Extension: could this work the other way around too? Try creating an ugly, threatening place and then add a beautiful, pristine object that doesn't belong there. Where might your story go next?

ACTIVITY 29. ON THE MOVE

Narrative momentum (noun): a quality of dramatic and engaging forward movement in a story.

When we're under pressure or in a rush, our imagination might conjure up a static scene – one that feels still and lacks movement. We might respond to a picture of a storm by creating a static scene at a bedroom window, with a character watching the rain come down. Or a picture of a beach might call up a sleeping sunbather. If we're not careful, our writing ends up without any sense of movement.

If you're writing a static scene that seems to lack life and drama, one solution is to swap it for a moving scene by switching your characters to the inside of a moving vehicle.

Example: Two characters argue. One feels the other has betrayed their friendship by concealing a piece of important news. They stand facing each other in the kitchen. Their conversation becomes heated.

Here the static, domestic setting could potentially rob the scene of its drama. A solution might be to move your characters through their surroundings, bringing in the sights and sensations of that movement into the conflict.

Choose one of the following moving locations:

- An overnight sleeper train with small rooms, bunk beds and a window looking out over the countryside speeding by.

- The back of a swiftly driven car, the city flashing past as the characters talk.

- A series of treetop walkways set up by an outdoor pursuits company – you must constantly move from challenge to challenge. Include zip wires, cargo nets, monkey bars and so on.

- The windy deck of a cross-channel ferry, sea spray misting the deck and gulls cawing overhead.

- A small boat with an outboard motor moving across a lake.

- A transatlantic flight shuddering through turbulence, the cabin lights flickering as an electrical storm rages.

- One character pulls another in a sledge. (Is the character being pulled injured?)

- A ski lift, suspended high over snowy slopes, moving slowly upward through the cloud.

- A canal boat chugging across a high viaduct hundreds of feet above a river valley.

- A moving container truck, the characters buffeted about in the back.

Adjust any element of the setting you like – the weather, time of day, size, shape or speed of the vehicle – until it provides an element of interest or drama. Or, if you prefer, create your own moving location.

Now you're ready to write.

Aim for 400 words in which two characters debate or argue – one has lied (or withheld information) from the other. It might be about a new friendship, an affair, a secret or some sort of betrayal.

Keep the scene enclosed, using your moving location. Shift between the description of the location – capturing a sense of movement – and the dialogue. Try to switch at dramatic or interesting moments. Use the movement to raise the tension. Cover only a small amount of time.

Close the scene with a line of vivid description about the moving landscape or a single line of powerful dialogue.

ACTIVITY 30. NOT WORLD-BUILDING

World-building (noun): the process of creating a consistent and realistic imaginary world.

All stories take part in a world of some sort. Fantasy and science fiction stories are famous for their other-worldly settings. An author in either of these genres could spend more time thinking up the rules of the world in which the story is set than the story itself. The logic of this world has to be true. For example, a world ruled over by reptiles for thousands of years will look very different to our own: walls may act as pavements if the reptiles are able to cling to rock faces. This would affect the architecture and appearance of cities; if, indeed, there are any cities – would reptiles need them? All of this needs to be thought through.

Other stories are set in historic worlds. Again, an author could spend a long time researching the clothing, language, customs and events of a certain time just to make sure that their story is realistic and accurate.

Setting your story in a modern world that you already know can save a lot of time – but that's what everyone else does too, so it may lose impact. Luckily, there are other ways to establish a setting quickly without limiting yourself or designing a bizarre reptile city. Your work might seem fresh and different if you take one of the following shortcuts. Of course, nothing beats careful and painstaking research, but these may help if you are writing under time constraints.

Set your story at a significant, well-known time in history

Start by considering the sinking of the *Titanic*, 9/11, the shooting of a famous politician or a particular battle during the Second World War. Or consider events even further back in history – the fall of a particular empire, the discovery of a country or the establishing of a trade route. You might use the arrival of a prophet or the crucifixion.

Now consider a character who might be one of history's bystanders. For example, if your character is a pickpocket who arrives in the crowded city of Bethlehem on a certain 'special' night, what happens next? Do they meet some wise men laden with treasure?

◼ Consider a historical period with distinctive music, cars and fashion

Next time you are in a crowd of people have a look around. Do you notice what most people wear? They don't stand out unless they have a striking haircut or are wearing something different. If your character is in 1950s New York, for example, she will be just the same. She won't really notice how people are dressed or what hairstyles they have unless they are unusual for the time.

However, if your character heard Buddy Holly playing on the jukebox in the soda bar on the corner of 9th Street and then mentioned a Chrysler parked nearby, then the reader might be able to get a sense of the time and place. A quick search on the internet should give you three things particular to a certain time, so your research doesn't have to be exhaustive.

◼ Technology and future settings

You can skirt around the whole world-building thing by choosing enclosed locations. A futuristic sci-fi backdrop can be made manageable if you set all the action on a spaceship. Ordinary domestic settings can be transformed by hinting at technological differences.

Imagine that the world doesn't change much from the way it is now, except that cars might be more fuel efficient or powered differently and people might listen to a different kind of music. The secret is not to get bogged down in too much explanation. These things could just be mentioned in passing: 'Nima told her entertainment pod to change tune. She hated the scratchy, grinding sound of Nu-scrape music.'

Once you've decided on your period in history (or the future), you're ready to write.

Present your reader with a vivid description of a character in a place. Make sure your character is doing something – your scene must be driven forward with action. Begin scattering your work with references to your setting. Drop in the details bit by bit.

Aim for 400 words. Focus on a single chosen location and cover only a small amount of time. Focus about 50% of your writing on the location and the other 50% on your central character and what they're doing.

CHAPTER 5

CRAFTING SHAPE AND STRUCTURE

SHAPE AND STRUCTURE

I am in blood

Stepp'd in so far, that, should I wade no more,

Returning were as tedious as go o'er.

Macbeth, 3.4: 142–144

This is the midpoint in Shakespeare's play. Macbeth has had Banquo murdered but Fleance, his son, has escaped. Macbeth realises at this moment that he is a monster, and that gaining redemption would be so big a task that he may as well wade on through the blood. The tragic hero has reached a point of no return and it's all downhill from here.

Books, films and TV programmes all have a structure. Many Hollywood blockbusters follow Blake Snyder's fifteen-beat structure outlined in his bestselling book *Save the Cat!*[1] Some critics might say that is why all these films seem the same. Nonetheless, in gaining sympathy for the main protagonist and cranking up the tension, the structure works.

Structure indicates a certain level of self-consciousness, planning and awareness of the audience – it's about pattern. We like the final scene of *Harry Potter and the Philosopher's Stone* because Harry has status and a new Hogwarts family, whereas he started the story as a bullied nobody who slept under the stairs in his uncle's house. The two images bookend each other. A search through the book would no doubt find a midpoint at which Harry commits to his life at Hogwarts and realises he has to stop Voldemort.

---

1   Blake Snyder, *Save the Cat! The Last Book on Screenwriting You'll Ever Need* (Studio City, CA: Michael Wiese Productions, 2005), p. 70.

Some writers will tell you that they don't plan – they just write by the seat of their pants. That's brilliant for them. We have no statistics or research to back this up, but we guess that such writers or 'pantsers' are probably slower writers than planners. Often, pantsers also have the luxury of time to write. With a few exceptions, every writer we know has opted for planning once they have a deadline to meet.

A carefully plotted piece of writing is a satisfying read. The reader innately senses the structure, the writing draws them in and sets them down once the piece has finished. There is a definite sense of closure – the reader knows that the piece has ended. Furthermore, a strong structure enables the writer to build in other elements such as foreshadowing and character change.

Well-structured narratives often get noted in examination feedback reports. Examiners seem to like circular tales or stories that have a structure that somehow mimics their subject matter. At the very least, a clear beginning, middle and end goes down well.

This chapter will give your students a number of different tricks and tools for creating coherently structured stories.

ACTIVITY 31. BASIC STRUCTURE – LOCATION, ACTION, CONSEQUENCE

Three-act structure (noun): a model that divides a story into three parts.

Planning and structure travel hand in hand: if you write a plan you are, at a simple level, mapping out a beginning, a middle and an end. This is a good place to start, especially when writing what is essentially short fiction.

An anecdote or a story from your past is useful material because it draws on your real experiences. You might find it hard to think of a single event you think is worth writing about, but it can be helpful to focus on a fairly ordinary event to begin with – for example, the first time you were told off by a teacher, the temporary loss of a pet, or a (non-traumatic) fall or accident.

Sometimes, it's hard to map out a story's beginning, middle and end, but if you write down the three main events of the story you can do this almost without thinking. You can develop your writing by including a location sentence (where did the anecdote happen?), an action sentence (what happened?) and a consequence sentence (what was the result?).

The beauty of this simple approach is that it creates a single piece with a strong concept. If you can sum up a story in a few sentences, then you know it won't run out of control and become too sprawling on the page. This is important for writing in short form. If you tell your story, verbally, and it becomes a rambling tale full of anecdotes, hundreds of characters and side plots, then you are never going to finish the story satisfactorily in class. If you can sum up the story in three simple sentences, then it will be easy to write quickly and develop.

Here is an example:

> Once, when I was about six or seven, I was playing in the sandpit at school with my friend, Alan Thomas. Without thinking, I picked up a handful of sand and threw it in his face. He went and told the dinner ladies, who took me to the head teacher. I stood outside the head teacher's office for the rest of lunch.

If we break that into three main events it looks like this:

Location (beginning): I sat in the school sandpit.

Action (middle): I threw sand in Alan's face.

Consequence (end): I was told off by the head teacher.

Once you have those three sentences you can write at any length, using description, dialogue, metaphor, foreshadowing or any of the techniques you need to bring the scene to life. It can be three paragraphs or three pages long.

Now it's time to write.

Your aim will be to write an entire story in 300 words. Use the location-action-consequence structure. This works best for personal anecdotes or memories, so you might want to begin with a story from your own life. Try 'A mistake I made', 'A bad decision' or 'A time when things went wrong' to generate an idea. On the other hand, you might want to stick to an entirely fictional narrative. That's OK too.

Make sure you're only covering a single event – don't try to cover too much action or time.

Remember to focus on your central characters and what it is they want. Make sure there is an element of conflict.

Use dialogue at some point in your story.

Extension: you might consider trying to shorten your story further. Can you do it in 150 words? Fewer? If you do an internet search for 'the shortest stories ever' you'll find loads of examples of fascinatingly short stories. Some writers claim they can tell a story in fewer than ten words. They're worth checking out!

ACTIVITY 32. WORKING BACKWARDS – PART 1: CONFLICT, CONFLICT, GOAL

Three-act structure (noun): a model that divides a story into three parts.

Author and blogger Nathan Bransford has a really useful and simple formula for a one-sentence pitch. We've found it helpful when we're thinking about structure. Bransford suggests this:

> When OPENING CONFLICT happens to CHARACTER(s), they have to OVERCOME CONFLICT to COMPLETE QUEST.[2]

Like location-action-consequence in Activity 31, Bransford's method suggests three parts, although they are a little more detailed. They are:

1. **The opening conflict**: Often referred to as an 'inciting incident', this is the something that begins the story.

2. **The obstacle**: In a full novel this would take up many pages; in a shorter piece this might be the main action we read about.

3. **The quest**: As a result of the central conflict, our character succeeds or fails – they reach or almost reach their goal. Either way, they learn something and change as a result.

This seems fairly straightforward, except that to make it work we need to know what our character wants to achieve. We've found that working backwards is a good way to do this. Here's how:

1. Begin with your character: what does my character want to achieve? Why is it important?

   Make notes here. Refer back to previous activities if you need to, or use Hearts and Clubs (Activity 10) to generate a character who wants something straight away.

2. Then decide on your ending: are they successful? If so, how does my story need to end?

---

2   Nathan Bransford, 'How to Write a One Sentence Pitch', *Nathan Bransford* (20 May 2010). Available at: https://blog.nathanbransford.com/2010/05/how-to-write-one-sentence-pitch.

Scribble some ideas down here. What exactly is that final scene going to look like? Play it through in your head. What will your character have learned? How will they have changed?

3. Then ask: what is the one main thing they need to overcome in order to reach this final scene? How has it been challenging? What conflict have you put them through?

    Make notes of what has happened immediately before the ending – the drama and conflict that might have taken place just before we reach the end of the story.

Once you've got these thoughts and ideas together, it's time to write.

Your aim will be to write the closing 300 words of a piece – your story's final scene.

Make sure the levels of conflict and drama are high, and then push your story through to its conclusion.

Remember to focus on your central character – their emotional response to this final scene will be important. Are they drained, exhausted, defeated or broken? Are they disappointed, sad or bewildered? Or are they filled with energy and positivity?

ACTIVITY 32

ACTIVITY 33. WORKING BACKWARDS – PART 2: CHARACTER WANTS AND STRUCTURE

Character arc (noun): the transformation undergone by a character during the course of a story.

If you've been doing these activities in order, you'll know that characters in a story always want something. That need is what drives them on. If your character doesn't want something or have some kind of goal, they will be passive – things will happen to them and the story will feel dull.

A character with an overriding need will drive a story along, and if the need is obvious and important to the character, the reader will invest some emotion in the character and enjoy the story.

Needs can be simple, such as wanting to find something – the Golden Fleece or the Philosopher's Stone – or they can be more complex and emotional – wanting to be liked or to have a family. In longer fiction a character may have several needs or goals, and they may conflict. In shorter fiction there may be one or two goals. The most important point is that the character changes.

Stories in which the character changes are satisfying reads but they are hard to write. These are generally stories that are confined to the personal anecdote genre. In the exam it might be, 'Think of a time when …'

If you have a good idea then the character change can structure your story. Here are the three steps:

1. Think how you want your character to be in the *end*: brave? Honest? Reunited with someone? Wiser about something?

2. Start the story as the *complete opposite of this*. If your character is finishing the story brave then they are a coward to begin with; if they end the story honest then they are a criminal at the start.

3. Then you have to think of an event that changes them.

In the context of a personal anecdote, think of three things and write them down. Here's an example:

1. When I was six, I hated Charli Jones. She always wanted to play with the same teddy bear in school as I did.

2. One day, she grabbed the head and I grabbed the legs. We pulled and it ripped apart. We were both upset.

3. Because of this we became best friends.

Look for the character change in the above example. What we're seeing here is a character who learns something – realising that their conflict destroyed what they both wanted. They're a changed person by the end, perhaps a little wiser.

Now it's time to write.

> Your aim will be to write an entire story. You've got 300 words to do it, so you'll need a single action and location. Don't try to include too much.
>
> Using the example above as a guide, design a three-part structure that focuses on character change. You'll need to create a main character who grows and changes as the result of an event. Draw on your own experience to give your story real meaning and depth. If you can't think of anything, stay fictional – but bear in mind that some fictional ideas might be a little too obvious. Skip past your first two or three ideas if they seem pretty common and well used.
>
> Remember to focus on your central characters – what it is they want. Make sure there is an element of conflict.
>
> Use dialogue at some point in your story.

ACTIVITY 34. NINE TYPES OF CHARACTER CHANGE

Dynamic character (noun): a character who undergoes an important inner change, such as a shift in attitude or personality.

As the previous activity has hopefully shown, a satisfying story often has character change at its heart. The reader meets the main protagonist in an innocent state, they travel together through an experience and the reader sees how the protagonist changes. If we manage to achieve this, we have – as the definition above suggests – a dynamic central character.

But how, exactly, might a character change?

In its simplest form, a character change story could be a morality tale – a character's bad experiences are used to warn off the reader from following the same path. Modern audiences are very wary of these kinds of stories, but other variants are hugely popular. In terms of satisfaction, the payoff for the reader of a changed character can be huge.

With a little thought we can hone our own anecdotal experiences into one of these tales. Inexperienced writers who might struggle with creating whole new fictional worlds or delving into history might find their own personal experience more accessible. Obviously, in real life people rarely learn clean and simple lessons from one experience, so guidance is needed to make the writing a distillation of experiences or maybe even a complete fabrication.

The strength of this approach is that the writer begins the story with a clear end point: the main protagonist is going to make herself sick of strawberry milkshake or overcome her fear of rollercoasters. This makes planning easier because you know where the story is going.

Again, a three-part approach to planning will work here: if your character is afraid of rollercoasters at the end of the story, she is going to be unafraid of them at the start. A rollercoaster ride in the middle is inevitable – something happens there that changes everything. A location-action-consequence plan might look like this:

Location – frame of mind (beginning): I stood in the queue for the rollercoaster.

Action – change happens (middle): The rollercoaster broke down and I was trapped for four hours.

Consequence – opposite frame of mind (end): Now I'm terrified of rollercoasters.

Below is a list of nine story archetypes. There are probably many more but these will serve as possible starting points for your next piece.

1. **The lesson learned**: These are moral tales. 'From that moment, I learned not to judge a book by its cover.' If not handled carefully these stories can become twee and obvious, but with a little thought they can be powerful tales.

2. **The repulsion story**: These are stories of greediness and excess. 'I'll never eat another chocolate caramel until the day I die.' These kinds of stories lend themselves to humour. Bill Naughton's short story 'Seventeen Oranges' is a great example of this.

3. **The tragic guilt story**: These are stories in which the writer is tormented by a memory of something they could have stopped but didn't. 'It was all my fault' or 'It wasn't my fault.' These are gripping stories as they take on the tone of confession and can have twists in them.

4. **The fear defeated story**: Self-explanatory, really. 'From that day on I never worried about X again.' This story can be inverted quite readily to explain a fear that has been held ever since that terrible experience.

5. **The smug secret story**: The protagonist wins some kind of secret victory over a bully or authority figure. 'To this day, I smile when I think of the expression on his face.'

6. **The comedy guilt story**: The protagonist is tempted to steal something they covet, but it turns out to be a gift for them anyway or maybe even theirs to begin with. They go through all the emotions of guilt, and maybe even confess, before realising their mistake. 'I thought I'd stolen it, but it was mine all along!'

ACTIVITY 34

7. **The victory story**: This is an anecdote about a time that the writer won. 'It was the best day of my life!' Students who enjoy sports often like to write these stories, but the key is to give the protagonist a disadvantage at the start – a physical one like a sprained ankle or a psychological one like a bullying teacher or friend who puts the character under huge pressure.

8. **The worm turns story**: These are related to victory stories but centre around an oppressed character. They might be fearful, bullied or beaten in some way, but then they rise to confront their oppressor. 'He never took my dinner money again.' These can be positive or sinister. It's even more interesting if the oppressed becomes the oppressor – the bullied becomes the bully.

9. **The horror story**: The classic encounter with dark, supernatural forces: ghosts, vampires, werewolves, ancient evil shadows. 'I never slept properly again.' The secret of these stories is that the narrator begins life as a sceptic. They might be rational and logical people who don't believe, but they're forced to change their opinions by the end. Less is more in these stories: blood and gore are spectacle, not horror!

Choose one of the examples above to frame your story. You can deviate from the examples given if you prefer. You might want to mash up two of these, or combine a couple in an interesting or unusual way. It's up to you.

Once you've decided which one to go for, you're ready to write.

> Your aim will be to write an entire story. You've got 300 words to do it, so you'll need a single action and location. Don't try to include too much.
>
> Remember to focus on your central characters – what it is they want. Make sure there is an element of conflict.
>
> Use dialogue at some point in your story.

ACTIVITY 35. WHAT, SO WHAT, THEN WHAT – PART 1

In medias res (adverb): beginning in the middle of events, starting without preamble or introduction.

The structure activities so far have encouraged you to think of stories that happen in three parts. But what if we're writing really short pieces? Perhaps it's possible to write a two-part story by beginning it after the first part has happened.

Many students facing the pressure of exam conditions decide to begin in the place that feels most natural – the opening of a day. Thus examiners and teachers end up reading a huge number of stories that open with an alarm clock going off.

Have a look at the following openings to stories, all genuinely written by Year 11 students. Of the six, we think two clearly stand out as stories that have the advantage of beginning in a good place. We hope it's pretty obvious which ones they are!

1. Bang! I jumped out of bed and quickly scoured the room for the source of the noise …

2. I was awoken by the cold penetrating my quilt.

3. It was a dark gloomy night in October, and I was walking home from a friend's house.

4. It was a dark Tuesday morning. My alarm was pounding.

5. It was another day. I woke up to the sounds of people talking and having fun outside.

6. The sound of silence fell upon me. Nervously, I stood waiting for my mum to pick me up. Every direction I looked there was dark forest surrounding me.

Four of the six students chose to begin their stories with a character in the first person waking up in bed. The other two immediately spring out as different and better. Why? Because things have happened *before* the opening of these stories. Using number 6 as an example, we can see how before the story started the character must have woken up, got dressed, had breakfast and possibly gone to school, and is now somewhere mysterious and interesting.

Even if your character is a courageous dragon slayer facing the biggest battle of their lives, your story would be dull if you told us about them waking up, getting out of bed and brushing their teeth.

Let's imagine that a story has three parts, but this time we're going to call them the 'what', the 'so what' and the 'then what'.

In this activity we're going to suggest you start at 'so what' and ignore 'what'. Have a look at the explanation below:

- **What**: This happens before the story starts. There's been a problem before your story begins. Your story has started because of this first 'what'.

- **So what**: The first 'what' has created issues. These are the 'so what'. Characters might be feeling something, forced to do something, scared of something or stressing about something. Your story begins here.

- **Then what**: As your character is worrying about the first 'what', add your 'then what' – another event. This makes things even worse.

In other words, you begin the story *after* something has already happened. Have a look at our worked example:

- **What**: Two friends, Nathan and Raine, have a go at online poker using Nathan's mum's credit card. They have a superb early win – £100. This makes them brave. They've since lost it all and stolen a further £50 from Raine's older brother to gamble. They've lost that too.

- **So what**: They're scared and desperate for money. There's a big poker night with a £1,000 pot for the winner starting at midnight. But Raine's brother Jed has found out about the lost money and is on the warpath. Rather than play from home, Nathan and Raine are crossing the park and heading for school, where they plan on breaking in to use the computers.

- **Then what**: *This is up to you!*

In this case, the story would open in the park at the 'so what' point. By this point, the two friends have woken up, had breakfast and done all the dull daily things we don't want to read about. The stakes are already high and the reader will quickly realise there's something important happening.

Of course, your challenge here is to make sure that you suggest what has happened before the story starts so we're not left confused. You might do this through dialogue or a quick reference to what has come before.

Choose one of the following tasks:

1. Begin writing the story outlined above.
2. Create your own set of characters and circumstances. Make a note of your 'what' and 'so what', and be sure to begin your story at 'so what'.

Once you've chosen, it's time to write.

> Aim for 400 words in total. Keep your scene enclosed, using only your single chosen location. Cover a small amount of time – up to twenty minutes of action.
>
> Consider closing the scene with a paragraph introducing the 'then what': finish by throwing another problem at your main characters.

ACTIVITY 36. WHAT, SO WHAT, THEN WHAT – PART 2

In medias res *(adverb): beginning in the middle of events, starting without preamble or introduction.*

As mentioned in the previous activity, many students facing the pressure of exam conditions decide to begin in the place that feels most natural – the opening of a day. You need to avoid that: it's done by huge numbers of students and often results in dull writing.

Let's remind ourselves: the start of each story has three parts – the 'what', the 'so what' and the 'then what'. Your job is to start at the 'so what' and ignore the 'what'. (For a quick explanation of this refer to Activity 35.)

In this activity we're going to give you a story in a series of numbered points. We've adapted this exercise from Jerome Stern's excellent *Making Shapely Fiction* – a book you should check out if you want to quickly improve as a writer of narrative fiction![3]

Here is a numbered description of what happens in a short story involving two characters, Mitchell and Eve. Read it through:

1. Mitchell meets Eve at work. He admires Eve, who seems daring, adventurous and outdoorsy.

2. Eve suggests they go deer hunting. On a misty autumn morning they drive through the countryside in Eve's truck.

3. In a tangle of forest Eve spots a deer, and together with Mitchell they approach.

4. Eve shoots the deer.

5. Then she approaches the deer's body and shoots it again, needlessly, another six times.

6. Mitchell realises there is something seriously wrong with Eve.

---

3   Jerome Stern, *Making Shapely Fiction* (New York: W.W. Norton, 2000), p. 41.

7.   They get back into Eve's truck. Eve chats casually as they drive home; Mitchell is silently terrified. It's awkward.

In the activity you're going to have to do three things:

1.   If you were panicking you might choose to begin this story at the start of a day: the alarm clock goes off, Mitchell gets out of bed … Not this time! Split the story into three sections – the 'what', the 'so what' and the 'then what'.

2.   Now decide which number (from 1–7) represents the precise point where you think this story would begin best. (Tip: it shouldn't be the 'what'.)

3.   Check your choice with other students. It doesn't have to be the same. Discuss the various options, change your mind if you want to and be ready to justify your choice!

You should now be ready to write.

Aim for 400 words in total. Be sure to begin at what you consider to be the correct point – and remember, there are a number of options here. It doesn't matter if yours is different from other people's.

Think carefully about the narrative point of view you're going to choose. Do we see the story from Eve's point of view? Or Mitchell's? Or are you going to write in the third person from outside the main characters?

Keep your scene enclosed, using only one chosen location.

Cover a small amount of time – perhaps one or two of the numbered points in the list.

ACTIVITY 37. SIMPLE TRY/FAIL CYCLES

Try/fail cycle (noun): a series of events that occur as a story's main character attempts to resolve their primary problem.

In many ways, it's the job of the writer to decide what their character wants and then prevent them from getting it for as long as possible.

Writers often refer to these 'blocking sections' as try/fail cycles. A try/fail cycle is a series of scenes in which a main character who clearly wants something attempts to get it, but can't. Often the cycles are repeated in a number of different ways. Each time they fail, but each time they learn. Three cycles is often enough for a simple story.

Here are two examples:

WANT: A CHARACTER WANTS DESPERATELY TO ASK ANOTHER CHARACTER OUT ON A DATE

Attempt 1: They talk in the corridor at school. Our main character nearly plucks up the courage to ask but can't quite do it.

Attempt 2: The two characters meet in different circumstances. Our main character nearly pops the question, but then the second character admits they're already going out with someone.

Final attempt: The two characters are asked to work together to complete a task (school work? Job outside of school?) and our main character eventually asks in an awkward stumbling way. They are politely rejected. The story ends with them learning something or changing in some way.

If we were making a movie, this story could go on for many try/fail cycles, but since we're focused on short narratives three is enough.

WANT: A CHARACTER HAS HAD THEIR PHONE CONFISCATED AND DESPERATELY WANTS TO GET IT BACK

Attempt 1: The character tries to sweet-talk the school office staff into letting them have it back, but a super-strict staff member realises they're being played. The phones are locked in the school safe until they're due to be returned.

Attempt 2: The character manages to get the code to the safe and sneaks into the office after school. But the safe is now empty.

Final attempt: The character asks someone else to steal it on their behalf but ends up getting the wrong phone. Perhaps they learn to rethink their obsession with their own phone. Maybe they return the phone to its owner and feel better about themselves.

Now design a few try/fail cycles of your own. You might want to use these examples to get you thinking:

- A character who needs to perform a note-perfect audition in one week's time.
- A character who has to find their kidnapped child.
- A character who wants to change their group of friends.
- A character who wants to break up with someone.
- A character who wants to give £1,000 to the most deserving person they know.
- A character who wants to give up social media.

Once you've decided what your character wants, your story will emerge by designing a simple try/fail cycle. They make three attempts to get what they want, leading up to a dramatic final scene in which they either succeed or fail.

Attempt 1: What happens? What does the main character learn?

Attempt 2: What happens? What does the main character learn?

Attempt 3: What finally happens? What does the main character learn?

Now that you've got a quick summary of what your character wants and how they're going to fail, you're ready to write a scene.

> Write from the perspective of the character who wants.
>
> Choose either the first, second or third section of the try/fail cycle. Your aim will be to write one scene of about 300 words. Don't try to include too much.
>
> Remember to focus on your central character – what it is they want. Make sure there is an element of conflict as you give them a particular setback to deal with.
>
> Keep the scene enclosed, using one single location.
>
> Use dialogue at some point in your story.

ACTIVITY 38. ADVANCED TRY/FAIL CYCLES: THE STORY PRE-MORTEM

Pre-mortem (noun): a strategy in which a failure is imagined and then worked back from to discover the cause of the failure.

The term 'project pre-mortem' was coined by psychologist Gary Klein and is widely used for project management in business and even the armed forces.[4] It might sound unusual but it's the opposite of a post-mortem: an analysis to determine why something died.

In a project pre-mortem you anticipate all the ways in which a project might end badly. The leader of the project outlines the most important goals for the future, and then invites their team to imagine that the project has failed. Each member of the team must think of a different reason why the project has been unsuccessful. What could possibly have sunk it? The leader collects the ideas and builds ways to avoid these failures into the project.

From a storytelling perspective this can be a really useful tool. It helps us to consider the conflicts and problems at the heart of a good story. If we imagine a story as a journey sparked off by a character's wants or needs, followed by a series of attempts to succeed, each attempt failing until the final success, then we can apply the pre-mortem process to story planning.

STORY PRE-MORTEM

A story pre-mortem might work like this.

The leader presents a character, outlining the character's wants and needs. They also provide the setting.

The team think of as many different ways as possible that the character may fail. These can range from death to delay or disappointment. The point is that the writer does not have to accept all of them, but by thinking about the options they can plan a story drawing from a long list of possibilities.

---

4   Gary Klein, 'Performing a Project Premortem', *Harvard Business Review* (September 2007). Available at: https://hbr.org/2007/09/performing-a-project-premortem.

The story grows out of how the character avoids some or all of these failures. Getting out of the most dangerous will make for an exciting read!

You can play the role of the leader or you can be in a team.

Here's an example:

- Character: Jay – a twelve-year-old boy who lives in a tall apartment block.
- Wants: To find his lost dog, Chewy.
- Setting: A city during a zombie apocalypse.

List the ways in which Jay could fail. You don't have to use all of them in the story – you're looking for as many options as possible.

Jay could:

- Find Chewy's devoured remains.
- Be eaten by his zombie family.
- Get lost in the city.
- Fall ill.
- Be attacked by a group of scavenging survivors.
- Fall into an abandoned lift shaft and die.
- Become a zombie and eat Chewy.
- Get electrocuted by a malfunctioning security fence and die.
- Hear a distant bark beyond an uncrossable river.

Let's consider these options under two headings:

1. **Final failures**: Obviously, some options are going to be better for continuing the story. If Jay steps out of the front door and is eaten by his little brother, then the story will be short and disappointing. These final failures kill the story completely – the character can no longer achieve their goal. You might want to use one, but not too early on!

2. **Continuity failures**: If Jay gets lost in the city, that is an interesting plot point because it will allow the story to continue. Continuity failures function as dramatic setbacks that make the central character work harder to achieve their goal.

Look at the list of failures and decide which ones will help the story to continue – mark them with 'CF'. Then look at the other failures that seem final and mark them 'FF'.

You should end up with something like this:

- Find Chewy's devoured remains. (FF)
- Be eaten by his zombie family. (FF)
- Get lost in the city. (CF)
- Fall ill. (CF)
- Be attacked by a group of scavenging survivors. (CF)
- Fall into an abandoned lift shaft and die. (FF)
- Become a zombie and eat Chewy. (FF)
- Get electrocuted by a malfunctioning security fence and die. (FF)
- Hear a distant bark beyond an uncrossable river. (CF)

Now look at the list of final failures. These don't have to be thrown away – they can be modified into 'near misses'. A near miss is when someone or something almost fails.

Finding Chewy's remains might become finding Chewy's collar with a speck of blood on it. Instead of being dead, Chewy might be alive. The final failure becomes a clue in the story. Similarly, if Jay is *nearly* eaten by his zombie little brother but manages to escape, this creates a point of tension that helps the story to progress.

Now we might have a list like this:

- Find Chewy's blood-stained collar. (NM)
- Be almost eaten by his zombie brother. (NM)

▨ Get lost in the city. (CF)

And so on. You should have more events in your list, but the next thing to do is put them into an order that makes for an exciting story.

Try it using our terrible zombie example. Pick three or four and sequence them in such a way that the action escalates, getting more dramatic each time.

In a sense, it is hard to get this wrong. We could have Jay finding the collar first, then encountering his zombie brother and then getting lost. We've chosen to do it this way because we think that finding the collar is a clue that would lead Jay to continue his search. (Your way may be different – and that's fine.)

▨ Be almost eaten by his zombie brother. (NM)

▨ Get lost in the city. (CF)

▨ Find Chewy's blood-stained collar. (NM).

How about considering some other starting points and developing a pre-mortem. Design your own or choose one of these two options.

OPTION 1:

▨ Character: A student on the school council obsessed with keeping her grades high.

▨ Wants: To attract the attention of the school bully who she secretly likes.

▨ Setting: A high achieving boarding school on a windswept moor.

OPTION 2:

▨ Character: A former thief who's decided to go straight.

▨ Wants: To return all the items they've stolen, one at a time.

▨ Setting: An inner-city academy.

Once you've decided on your starting point and run a decent pre-mortem you should have a sequence of failures. You're now ready to write.

> Your aim will be to write one scene of about 300 words. That means picking one of the things you've decided will happen – a single action – so try not to include too much.
>
> Remember to focus on your central characters – what it is they want. Make sure there is an element of conflict as you give them a particular setback to deal with.
>
> Use dialogue at some point in your story.

ACTIVITY 39. FAST FORESHADOWING

Foreshadowing (noun): A hint, indication or warning that something is going to happen in the future.

'Little did they know that trouble was just around the corner …'

This is an obvious (and clumsy) example of foreshadowing, and is best avoided, but it demonstrates what foreshadowing does. It shows that you are aware of your audience, that your story is leading towards something dramatic and tense, and that you are influencing your reader by referring to this event.

Foreshadowing involves careful planning or diligent redrafting. You can't fore-shadow if you don't know what is going to happen next. If you plan your story you can include the points you want to foreshadow as you write, and your story will appear much more sophisticated as a result. If you don't plan you will need to go back and rewrite sections to include foreshadowing once you have finished.

The best kind of foreshadowing involves inference. This is when you hint at something without actually stating it in words. When readers infer they draw conclusions that aren't clearly stated.

Here are five examples of foreshadowing. We've chosen these because they're quite easy to use. You may be able to come up with others or think of times when foreshadowing happens in books or films.

1. **The rhetorical question**: '"What could be easier?" Joe thought to himself …'

    In the statement above, the reader quickly realises that whatever Joe is about to do, it will be anything but easy. That's inference and foreshadowing.

2. **The 'we all knew' statement**: 'We all knew that, when using a chainsaw, it is essential to keep both hands on the machinery at all times. At least, I thought that we all knew that. Obviously, Helen didn't.'

    This kind of foreshadowing also uses inference. It is different because it hints more directly at the impending disaster and who the victim is going to be.

3. **The inclement weather**: 'Dark storm clouds gathered above the unfortunate village like a flock of hungry, impatient carrion crows.'

   Sometimes the foreshadowing can be even more subtle. It can be hidden away in the words you use to describe a setting. In this example, we know that something bad is going to happen to the village but it isn't clear what. Unlike the chainsaw example, in which we anticipate that the saw is going to be involved, we aren't certain how the 'unfortunate village' is going to meet its fate.

4. **The object**: 'Sasha opened the drawer and stared at the heavy outline that lay sleeping there. A gun.'

   Rather like the chainsaw, if your character sees a gun in a drawer it suggests that violence will occur somewhere in the story. The short sentence here emphasises the object's importance. Try using a similar technique yourself.

5. **The chance comment**: 'I hope you can be happy at Falcon Manor.'

   You'll need a second character to make the chance comment. You have a choice to make: the character could be genuinely well-meaning, which will produce one effect, or they could be sinister and slightly frightening, which will produce an entirely different effect. Either way, the comment suggests that the main character will find it difficult to be happy and hints at possible events in the story.

Further options:

6. **Subversion**

   Now you've considered the options above you can think about subverting them. It is possible to subvert foreshadowing, and this can fool the reader in a satisfying way.

   Think of Helen and her chainsaw. What if the disaster didn't happen to Helen as expected but to an innocent bystander? Or what if it isn't the chainsaw that causes the problem but that Helen gets her hand caught in another piece of machinery when she is reaching for something?

7. **Delayed gratification**

You may have heard about the Stanford Marshmallow Test in 1970.[5] In very simple terms, the test set out to establish the age at which children were able to wait for a reward. Children were given a plate with a marshmallow on it and told that if they waited for fifteen minutes before eating it, they could have a second treat. Obviously, some children couldn't resist the temptation to eat the marshmallow right under their noses, but many could.

Your foreshadowing is a bit like the marshmallow. You've made a promise that something is going to happen, but the longer you can hold off the terrible event, the more satisfying it is for the reader. In longer novels, the reader may have even forgotten about the foreshadowing and is only reminded of it when the fateful event occurs.

8. **The empty threat**

As with all so-called 'rules', there is always an exception. Sometimes, if you are writing a piece of atmospheric description, you might hint at something that will happen in the future just to create a sense of threat. The dark storm clouds mentioned earlier might be a good example of this.

Once you've decided on your foreshadowing technique, you're ready to write.

Your aim will be to write the opening scene of a story. Aim for 300 words.

You'll need one or two characters and one location, so keep your scene enclosed. Try to cover only a small amount of time.

Remember: using too much foreshadowing becomes exhausting for the reader and will make your writing feel amateurish. It is wise to foreshadow an event just once, or twice at the most.

---

5   See Janine Zacharia, 'The Bing "Marshmallow Studies": 50 Years of Continuing Research', *Stanford University Bing Nursery School* (24 September 2015). Available at: https://bingschool.stanford.edu/news/bing-marshmallow-studies-50-years-continuing-research.

EXTENSION: GUESS THE EVENT

Once you're done, you might benefit from letting someone else read your scene and give you some foreshadowing feedback.

Can your reader guess what is going to happen? Get them to rate your story using the table below.

1	Too obvious – I knew exactly what was going to happen.
2	I had some doubts but was still pretty sure what was going to happen.
3	I could tell something was going to happen and which character or object it might involve.
4	I understood the mood of the writing and that there was a threat, but it was unclear who was in peril.
5	I couldn't tell who was at risk or what was going to happen other than something bad.

Hopefully, you'll realise that a score of 3 or 4 is ideal. You don't want your foreshadowing to be too obscure and uncertain, and you don't want it to be so obvious that it robs your story of drama.

ACTIVITY 40. MIRRORING

Mirroring (noun): the repetition of an image or idea, often in its opposite form.

We can give shape to stories by mirroring or repeating events, actions or images. At the end of John Steinbeck's powerful novel *Of Mice and Men*, something happens to one of the main characters – and it's the exact same thing that has already happened to a dog in a previous chapter. The two events mirror each other, suggesting a connection and encouraging the reader to think and reflect.

Similarly, J. K. Rowling famously claimed that she had devised the final scene of the last Harry Potter book long before the series was finished. It was a mirroring of something that had happened much earlier in the series.

You're operating on a smaller scale, but you can do the same to give shape and structure to your writing. Could there be an image at the start that reappears at the end in a different way, encouraging the reader to see the connection and enjoy the story on a deeper level?

You might want to think about the following images. They're all pretty obvious – you could come up with many better ones. But they might provide a useful starting point for developing and exploring a possible start and end for your story.

At the beginning	At the end
A character lights a candle. (A hopeful image? New light? Insight, understanding and wisdom? Or the passing of time and the inevitability of death?)	The candle goes out and the room is plunged into darkness.

At the beginning	At the end
A character shuffles and deals a pack of cards. (An image about games of chance? Risk-taking? Hope and positivity – youthful games? Friendships?)	The character puts the cards away and places the pack in a drawer.
A character repeatedly ignores an incoming phone call. (An image suggesting fear? Not wanting to face up to responsibility? Avoiding conflict? Lacking courage or resilience? Wanting to avoid bad news? Prolonging the inevitable?)	The phone rings again. Finally, this time, the character answers it.
A character pours a beer and drinks it in one long gulp. (An image suggesting addiction? An inability to face life without alcohol? A response to some sort of trauma? Hiding from reality?)	The character orders a beer in a bar, then leaves it undrunk and walks out into the street.
A wild and violent storm rages. (An image suggesting violence and chaos? The power of nature? The unpredictability of fate? The inability of our characters to control their lives?)	It stops raining. Above a bank of cloud the sun appears.
A character constantly plays with a beaded necklace. (An image of anxiety and fear? Worry beads? Or a religious object linked with faith and belief?)	The character takes the necklace off and gives it to another character.

In order to choose your images or ideas, you might need to begin with your main character: who are they and what do they want? What are their aims and

ACTIVITY 40

172

goals? What are they trying to achieve during the course of the story? How are they going to change? Is there an image, object or idea that helps to convey that struggle or change? How might you incorporate it at the beginning and the end?

Once you've thought this through, you're ready to write an opening scene.

> Either begin a new story with an arresting image that you could mirror later on, or revisit the beginning of a story you've already completed and add the image you want to return to at the end.
>
> Aim for 300 words.
>
> If you can, keep the scene enclosed, using a single location.
>
> Emphasise the image so that the reader realises it is in some way important.

CHAPTER 6

EDITING

Ernest Hemingway is often credited with coining the now famous aphorism, 'The only kind of writing is rewriting.' It's a useful place to begin a chapter on editing: the activities in this chapter all assume that the student has a completed piece of work alongside them and is ready to begin to assess its strengths and weaknesses before embarking on their rewrite.

Of course, to reach this point a writer needs to have finished something. We can't stress how important it is to complete a piece of work. You'll find writing advice rife with exhortations to 'finish no matter what'. Martin and Jon have both spent wasted years tinkering with half-finished projects, partly because to never finish is to avoid judgement. Only when we had completed our first 60,000-word middle grade or young adult novel for the first time were we ready to take the next step. Students will, of course, feel the same urge to protect their ego – an impulse which often manifests itself in endlessly polishing an opening paragraph and never progressing.

Our first job is to push our students to finish. One complete terrible story beats fifty abandoned openings.

Once sitting with a complete piece, writers (Martin and Jon included) often pass through a blissful forty-eight-hour period where, psychologically speaking, the story is untouchably brilliant – the best thing they've ever written. We can't conceive of any negative feedback, can't imagine what any reader might find to criticise. Upon rereading it a couple of days later, however, it's awful. We need to give students the space to treasure a piece before we encourage them to make changes.

And when we do edit, it's worth being clear what we're looking for. We have witnessed students' resistance to editing because the focus of the edit is the minutiae of punctuation – those micro-adjustments to expression. Often, students aren't sure what to look for and give their work a cursory read-through, searching for spelling mistakes. If the focus is immediately on style, it means that students miss the point that paying attention to structure, tone and mood are just as important.

So, you might encourage a *structural edit*. (Do the right things happen in the best order?)

Or a *character edit*. (What does the central character want? How do they change?)

Or a *tonal edit*. (What colour do you want your story to be? How does your imagery support this?)

Or an *edit for pace*. (Where does this feel slow or sticky? Where does it gallop?)

Or you might go for a read-through – aloud – to consider the piece at a sentence level.

There are plenty of options, but we must resist the temptation to polish to perfection. We can unintentionally kill projects with endless edits. ('I never want to write another story *again!*') Instead, you might consider allowing or specifying only a limited number of changes to acknowledge the important psychological component to editing.

Whatever your approach, the message needs to be clear: first, finish. And once you're done, leaving enough time to edit can transform a short piece of writing. As professional writers, both Martin and Jon have learned over and over again the transformative power of good editing.

Unlike the activities in other sections of the book, the students might not want or need to consider all ten of these strategies. They might be aware enough to know the two or three they need to work through. Others might need to spend time completing one at length. Use them on a case-by-case basis.

ACTIVITY 41. SIX COMMON PROBLEMS

Here are six types of story writer we see a lot. Could it be that your writing has one or more of these problems? Have a look through a recent piece you've written and check.

1. **The outliner**

   The story is an outline of what happens, told as quickly as possible. Often, a lot happens; too much for a short story and enough for a couple of chapters of a novel or fifteen minutes of a movie. Sometimes, a full day, a few days, a week or a month is covered in the world of the story. There is no adjustment in the passage of time – all scenes pass equally quickly. This happened, then this, then this. Frequently there is no dialogue.

   Possible solution: Read a similar scene from a published prose narrative. Then choose one scene from your outlined story and magnify it. Try The Magnified Moment (Activity 48).

2. **The list-maker**

   The physical dimensions of each character are precisely listed as if they are taking part in an experiment. We know very little about them except that they are 6 feet and 2 inches tall with dark brown hair cut into a side parting to the left, and their waist measurement is 34. They have size 9 shoes. Clothing brands are often added. Locations are also lists of objects.

   Possible solution: If characters are the problem, read a character description from a published prose narrative. Then try moving away from physical characteristics towards mannerisms or wishes. Try Wishes, Wants and Goals (Activity 11) or Character Tics (Activity 15). If locations are the problem, read a location description from a published prose narrative, and then adjust your writing. Try Making the Senses Work for You (Activity 23).

3. **The sales rep**

   Elements of persuasive writing enter description so the story sounds as if it is an advert for the food being eaten or the hotel at which the events take place.

   Possible solution: Read a similar scene from a published prose narrative. Copy it as closely as you can. Then check the two examples next to each other to see where you went wrong.

4. **The writer with no feelings**

When good things happen characters feel 'brilliant'. When bad things happen they are 'gutted'. When a place or event has sinister qualities they are 'scared'. When they are under great pressure they 'can't think straight'. Feelings and emotions are labelled rather than described, so we're told rather than shown.

Possible solution: Read a similar scene from a published prose narrative. Then try Killing the Word 'Was' (Activity 47).

5. **The bad simile user**

'I staggered to the mountaintop. Wind whistled past my ears, blowing snow in my face. I shivered. Up there on the hill it was as cold as ice cream.'

The first cold thing you can think of might not be the one that gives the effect you're looking for. Threatening scenes need threatening imagery.

Possible solution: Check out simile use in a published prose narrative – you might find there isn't much. Now try adjusting your similes using a mind-map. List twenty things that are cold, then choose the best one for the situation and circumstance you're describing.

6. **The punctuater**

'My heart was beating like a drum!! The old man was in fact my father!!!'

There is almost no reason to ever use an exclamation mark, unless in dialogue, and there is never a good reason to use more than one. Exclamation or underlining may well be a sign that your vocabulary or sentences need improvement.

Possible solution: Read a dramatic scene from a published prose narrative. Look at sentence length to see if that is being used to do the job of exclamation. Also look at dramatic vocabulary. Then try Where's the Tension? (Activity 46).

ACTIVITY 42. MOOD, AGENCY, CONFLICT – THREE CRUCIAL STORY STRANDS

Often, we read a story and it just goes nowhere, or it has plenty of description but lacks any kind of unity. It could be a shopping list for all the reader cares. Your story needs to be consistent throughout in terms of imagery; if you just scattergun images across the page, the effect of your writing is reduced. If your character doesn't want anything and simply stands passively observing, things become dull very quickly. If there is nothing hampering your character's need, the story is over before it begins.

Select a recent piece of writing you've completed and check it for three things: mood, agency and conflict. Try to make sure these three things occur three times in your story and at three points: beginning, middle and end.

MOOD, OR WHAT COLOUR IS YOUR STORY?

Every story has a mood. It might be upbeat, it might be sad or threatening. Colours are closely linked with mood. We associate greys, blacks, blues and purples with sadness; yellows and oranges are often said to be cheerful.

If you think of your story in terms of a colour, what colour would it be? At this point you might shrug and say, it's just neutral. *That*, then, is the problem. Your story can't afford to be neutral; if your story is neutral then your character has no feelings and your reader won't care. Pick a mood for your story – it might be the mood of the main character or of all the characters. Then pick a colour to go with it.

Once you've decided on the colour, think of three similes or metaphors that might fit the colour and mood. You might choose purple because your story has a feeling of threat about it. Then you might think of a simile: as purple as a bruise. Come up with other colours that match purple, blue, grey, black and create some more images.

The colour is only a starting point. It might be that the image of the bruise makes more sense in your story. You can add other forms of injury imagery too, such as a fracture or laceration.

If you want something to contrast with your image, you can think of the opposite. You may have a character who is bright and cheerful, so you could describe them differently to create a contrast.

What is most important is that your images are coherent and connect with each other. If your similes are as green as moss, as fast as a cheetah and as bright as lightning, they will feel artificial and forced (see 'The bad simile user' in Activity 41). If they are themed, they will create a sense of unity in your work.

AGENCY

According to Kurt Vonnegut, 'Every character should want something, even if it is only a glass of water.'[1] What does your character want? What is driving them forward? It doesn't have to be anything too deep or meaningful – it could be that they want to do their shopping but the weather is making it unpleasant. Make your character actively pursue something she wants or needs or your reader won't care about them.

If you are writing a description, perhaps prompted by a photograph, you still need your character to want something. It's their justification for surveying the scene. It's the reason they will move through the landscape.

There are lots of tips about characters' wants and needs earlier on in the book – check through Wants vs. Needs (Activity 12) or Mistaken Wants and the Moment of Realisation (Activity 13).

Make sure you reference what the character wants at the three points in your story. The character may achieve their goal at the end, or if you're writing a twist they may achieve something different but better. The character may also fail. This is still a way of referencing their need.

ACTIVITY 42

---

1   See Maria Popova, 'Kurt Vonnegut's 8 Tips on How to Write a Great Story', *Brainpickings* (3 April 2012). Available at: https://www.brainpickings.org/index.php/2012/04/03/kurt-vonnegut-on-writing-stories/.

CONFLICT

As we have seen, conflict is essential to any story. It adds interest to a description. If your writing seems flat and two-dimensional, it may be that the conflict isn't emphasised enough.

Conflict in this context is closely linked to the character's wants and needs. If your character needs to get out of a burning building, the conflict is going to arise out of heat, flames and falling debris. Mention them at different points in the story. If your character wants to get home from school, the conflict may arise from a gang of bullies intent on intercepting her. Have three escapes or near misses before she gets caught. If your character wants to steal some sweets from the local shop, it may be his better nature or fear of being caught that is stopping him. Maybe there are two failed attempts to approach the counter and take the sweets, followed by a successful third try.

Make sure you have conflict built into your story. The next activity might help you to do that!

ACTIVITY 43. ADDING CONFLICT

We've said this before: conflict is the lifeblood of stories. When we look through narratives that aren't working, it often comes down to conflict. It is either absent or very hastily described.

Remember, conflict doesn't mean all-out war or physical violence. It can be internal conflict or verbal conflict through argument or disagreement.

Or, as this activity suggests, it can be built into a description.

CONFLICT VERBS

You can inject conflict into your sentences to bring your story alive, but you have to use 'conflict verbs'. Conflict verbs are verbs that sound violent, threatening or dangerous! For example:

Fog swirled in the streets muffling all sound like cotton wool.

vs.

Fog crept through the streets, suffocating all sound.

You might recognise conflict verbs from the Instant Pathetic Fallacy (Activity 21). They are simply more powerful verbs.

Here is a useful list of conflict verbs:

- Hit, punched, beat, struck, flailed, whipped, thumped, slapped, smacked, pummelled, smashed.
- Strangled, smothered, suffocated, throttled, garrotted.
- Wrestled, clawed, struggled, tangled, battled.
- Stabbed, slashed, sliced, cut, wounded, carved, pinioned, hacked, gouged.
- Screamed, howled, yelled, roared, bellowed.

Clearly, all we have done here is give a list of synonyms for the first word in each row. It's not rocket science; if you have access to a thesaurus you can compile your own list of conflict verbs and learn them. You can then deploy them when you need to write in a hurry.

The passage below uses conflict verbs to create a sense of chaos out of a normal everyday scene. This is a great technique for building tension or creating a sense of desperation. You can use conflict verbs more sparingly to conjure up a less hectic setting.

I stared across the teeming playground, searching for Asif. A cold wind slapped my cheeks. Children screamed and charged around the playground, their laughter stabbing at my ears. A football smacked against the old brick wall of the school and bounced, thumping to the black tarmac. Then I spotted his green top. Battling towards him, I pushed back at kids shouldering into me, their faces blurred by speed. From somewhere, the smell of toast invaded my senses. A feeling of nausea slowly strangled me. The figure in green vanished. A jet roared overhead, carving white furrows in the blue sky. Out on the road, beyond the blue railings, lorries and car horns bellowed back. Where had Asif gone? Maybe I should ask the supervisor. She stood like a lighthouse in the stormy sea of schoolchildren who pummelled into each other around her. She lifted the silver whistle to her lips. Time was running out.

ACTIVITY 44. ABCDE

This activity gives you a simple tool for checking your writing. It helps writers to realise when their work needs adjustment – and often tells them what's missing. It's based on the premise that when we're writing a narrative, our sentences tend to do one of five things. Luckily, these five types of sentence begin with the letters A, B, C, D and E!

Action. The plot is pushed forward by something happening. Sometimes it might be dramatic: 'She struck out at the wild animal, swinging the spade before her like a weapon.' And sometimes it might be more subtle: 'She poured the coffee, filling it a little too much, and watched it steam.'

Background. The location is described: 'The distant trees seemed to shimmer in the afternoon light.'

Character. We learn more about a character in the story – their thoughts, ideas and motivations: 'Jack knew he wouldn't make it across the bridge. His fear of heights had started when he was very young and he'd never been able to overcome it.'

Dialogue. Someone says something to someone else and we indicate it with speech marks. It's often doing one of the other four things for us. Dialogue can be action: 'Put down the gun or you'll regret it!' Background: 'Is it always this cold here? I'm freezing!' And, of course, character: 'I don't trust you, Gabriel. I never have.'

Emotional response. You might be creating atmosphere, tension, fear or excitement: 'Her heart thudded hard against her ribs and sweat beaded at her temples.'

You'll quickly realise that the ABCDE model is a simplification; writing is much more complex than this. Sentences in stories are often doing many different things at once. For example:

> The figure stepped forward as the moon emerged from behind a ragged bank of cloud and shadows lengthened across the graveyard.

A sentence like this might be partly A (the figure stepping forward), partly B (the moonlight and the graveyard) and partly E (a sense of rising fear and anxiety.)

Nevertheless, we've found the model useful in figuring out if there's too much of something or too little. Read your work, label your sentences and work out if there's an imbalance. Here's an example to help you consider your own writing.

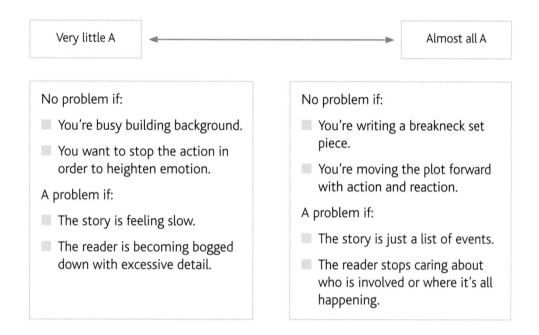

| Very little A | | | Almost all A |

No problem if:

- You're busy building background.
- You want to stop the action in order to heighten emotion.

A problem if:

- The story is feeling slow.
- The reader is becoming bogged down with excessive detail.

No problem if:

- You're writing a breakneck set piece.
- You're moving the plot forward with action and reaction.

A problem if:

- The story is just a list of events.
- The reader stops caring about who is involved or where it's all happening.

The same goes for B, C, D and E – each have their strengths and weaknesses, so you'll need to make a judgement about whether you have the balance right or not.

Here are five issues we've seen in the past. One of these might describe your current work:

1. **An over-reliance on action sentences so the story feels more like an 'outline'**

   That is, a summary of a film or book that goes: 'This happened, then this, then this.' Often, huge amounts of time pass very quickly in stories that feel outlined.

   Possible solution: Slow down time and concentrate on writing one magnified moment.

2. **A tendency to over-describe so that background and emotional response sentences dominate the story**

    The story might feel static or stuck, lacking movement and progress because a character is sitting on their bed thinking for long periods.

    Possible solution: Have a character make a decision and do something.

3. **No dialogue**

    There are characters and events but no one speaks directly to anyone else. Instead, dialogue is described as part of the story: 'I told her all about it and she replied saying she was sorry. Then we were at the school gates and we said goodbye to each other and agreed to meet later.' There's nothing wrong with this, particularly if the dialogue would have been pretty dull, but the result is often that we don't know the characters very well. We've never heard them speak.

    Possible solution: Insert a difficult conversation or argument to inject drama.

4. **No character sentences**

    These stories are often told in the first person, but we learn nothing of the character because they never reveal anything about themselves. Even when they're falling out with their best friend, it doesn't feel dramatic because we don't really know who they are or what they want from life.

    Possible solution: Decide what your character wants – their aims, goals and obsessions. Then begin to hint at them as the story goes on.

5. **Very limited background sentences**

    The story might have one or two: 'I arrived at the river's edge', then the rest of the story happens without any further reference to the location. The reader forgets where the action is taking place and it feels like it could be anywhere.

    Possible solution: Use the senses to conjure up a location, then remind your readers of where you are. Use an object from the location or an element of the location in the action of the story.

ACTIVITY 45. SCAMPER

The SCAMPER acronym is often used in design settings to encourage creative product design. Here, we've adjusted it so that it applies to stories. Whenever you're feeling that your story is missing something, or in some way deficient, try this activity.

Take each element of SCAMPER in the following table and check through the suggestions for what to do. Swapping is a simple one to consider. (The number of times we've injected new life into an idea by swapping the genders of characters is incredible!)

Choose three you might want to have a go at. Spend five minutes on each, really persisting with your thinking. (Even when your initial response is, 'This will never work!' it's worth pushing on. We've done this many times before and found it to be really helpful, even when it feels crazy.) By the end, you may have some new ideas or possibilities to develop.

If you don't, choose another three elements of the SCAMPER model and force yourself to take five minutes on each. These are the ones you didn't initially choose so this will be harder. Again – persist! You might emerge exhausted by the end of your fifteen minutes, but like last time there might be the beginnings of a new set of ideas.

Swap	Swap the roles of two characters – their positions or status. Or swap their genders or ages. See what happens. Swap the locations in which things happen to see if it feels fresher.
Clean up cliché	Examine your work for anything familiar or expected – a setting your reader will have seen before, a character they will be familiar with, a conversation or line of dialogue. Remove your clichés – then try to use 'reverse' or 'swap' to produce something more interesting.

Adapt	Take a section of your work you feel is weaker (Character? Plot point? Location?) and adapt someone else's idea into your work. Borrow a character from somewhere else and adapt them to fit. Borrow another location and adapt to fit ... and so on.
Magnify	Take something – a character, a place, an event – and make it twice as much as it was, or ten times as much. Magnify its drama in some way.
Pair up	Take two characters and turn them into one, pairing up their characteristics into a single person. Does this give you the space to add another character? Are there other characters who could be combined?
Eliminate	Take out an element of the story and check what happens. Persist with this, checking elements and removing them. Does the story improve as a result of eliminating something?
Reverse	Take an event or plot point and try to reverse it – make the opposite happen. Or take a character and make them the complete reverse of what you might have planned. Something entirely unexpected might emerge.

ACTIVITY 46. WHERE'S THE TENSION?

Tension is the build-up to something exciting, terrible or funny happening. It's the ride to the top of the rollercoaster, just before you go clattering down the steep bit.

In that moment at the top of the rollercoaster, the people in the cars can't see the drop – they are edging their way to the peak. They know that a drop is coming but they have to rely on their imagination to envisage it. People who design rollercoasters know that not being able to see something is a good way of making us imagine that the drop will be worse than it actually is.

Writers can use similar techniques to make their stories into rollercoaster rides. Examine a recent piece of work and see if you have employed any of the following techniques.

EMPTY WORDS

There was a reason that Stephen King entitled his bestselling novel *It*. The monster in the story can change itself into whatever you fear most. 'It' is an empty word. If we use the word 'it' or 'something', our reader fills in the meaning of that word with their imagination. Jokes use tension too: they withhold information, leaving the listener desperate to know how the story will end. That's what makes the punchline so rewarding – usually. In the same way, you can hold back on telling the reader what that 'something' is. If you say, 'A big, snarling werewolf scratched at the window', that is like telling the punchline of the joke first. There is no build-up. It's better to keep the reader guessing for at least a few sentences or paragraphs before you reveal the threat.

ONOMATOPOEIA

Rollercoasters are noisy for a reason. It adds to the tension. Every bump and clunk as you travel to the top of the ride is designed to make you mistrust the machine. By the time you've bumped your way to the top, you are convinced it is going to break and send you screaming to your death. Similarly, a sound effect can build tension. It might be breathing or a dripping tap. It might be someone drumming their fingers as they wait for you to tell the truth. Sound effects work.

THE RULE OF THREE

Isn't it strange how things seem to be grouped into threes? In fairy stories, public speaking, marketing and problem-solving, three seems to be the magic number. It isn't clear why we respond well to triads but it certainly works in writing. If you repeat an 'empty word' you can get away with it three times. Any more than that and it becomes a distraction. 'Something scratched at the door as I huddled by the fire. I could hear something snuffling outside. Something big.'

Similarly, you can repeat a sound effect: 'Something scratched at the door as I huddled by the fire. Scratch. Scrape. I could hear something snuffling outside. Something big. Scratch. Scrape.'

THE TICKING CLOCK

Sometimes a time limit can build tension. This could be a literal countdown: 5, 4, 3, 2, 1. It could be a reminder that there is only five minutes left before the hero's true love gets on the train and leaves. It could also be a distance count as someone runs: 'Twenty metres of station platform left. I can see her stepping up into the carriage …'

RHETORICAL QUESTIONS

Too many rhetorical questions can kill your work, but a strategically placed rhetorical question can have a huge impact and effect on your reader. They're best employed when they draw attention to something disturbing or strange, or when the character has a revelation: 'Who would leave a single glove in the middle of the kitchen floor? Then I noticed the finger of the "glove" twitch.'

ACTIVITY 46

ACTIVITY 47. KILLING THE WORD 'WAS'

This is a simple editing technique that can help with redrafting. 'Was' is the past tense of the verb 'to be'. It is often used when writing in the passive voice. This is the kind of writing used in scientific experiments or newspaper reports. It is designed to sound dispassionate and objective.

In action scenes, and when you are trying to create atmosphere, 'was' and other passive constructions can suck the life out of your writing. It also limits your options for expanding a sentence.

> It was raining.

This is a bald statement that nobody would use in their writing, but it is useful to illustrate the point.

If we decide what we are writing about (i.e. rain) and start the sentence with that word, then a more active sentence should follow.

> Rain ...

We now have to choose a verb to say what the rain does. Let's go for 'hammered'.

> Rain hammered ...

Then we have to say what it hammered on.

> Rain hammered on the tin roof.

Just by rephrasing the sentence and removing 'was', we've made a more active sentence, and it gives us a little more information about the setting or location.

Here are some other examples:

> Rain rattled on the hood of my coat.

> Rain turned the pond's surface into a stormy sea.

Have a go! Change two of these into more active sentences by removing 'was':

- It was cold.
- I was tired.
- It was dark.
- It was foggy.

EMOTIONS

In a similar way, getting rid of the word 'was' helps us to describe emotions in more detail. For example:

I was scared.

vs.

My heart thumped against my ribs. Sweat beaded my forehead and I clung, white-knuckled, to the safety rail.

Think of all the things that happen when you're scared: your heart rate speeds up, your hands become clammy, you sweat or shake, your eyes widen, your mouth gapes and you feel frozen to the spot.

These are the things you would feel *physically* if you were scared, or you might see in someone else if they were feeling fearful. Once you've generated a list, simply pick three of them and combine them into two sentences.

Have a go! Use the table on page 193 to make the following sentence more active and interesting:

I was afraid.

ACTIVITY 47

Symptoms of fear	
Sweat	Eyes widened
Hands trembled	Mouth hung open in shock
Breathing in short gasps	Knees felt like wet string
Heart pounded	My head spun
Stood frozen	My heart thumped
Held my breath	Blood pulsed around my temples
Shivered	I bit my lip
Scalp prickled	I put my hands to my face

This table will enable you to create a couple of go-to sentences that mean 'I was scared.' Each time you want to write, 'I was scared' you can deploy one of the sentences. Your writing will come alive as a result.

ACTIVITY 48. THE MAGNIFIED MOMENT

As a story writer you're a bit like a film director. You're going to choose which scenes we get to see and which end up on the cutting-room floor. And once you've chosen which scenes will be in your movie, you get to choose how we see them. Will there be music? Lighting effects? Slo-mo?

Let's apply that to prose stories.

Some unsuccessful stories feature the wrong scenes. We don't necessarily want to see the main character having breakfast; we want to get to the action instead. The wrong scenes are in the story and the wrong ones are on the cutting-room floor.

Other story writers choose the right scenes but then rush them. We don't get the moody music, the eerie lighting and the slowed-down time. We gallop through in a single sentence. If this is you, one solution is to magnify certain scenes. This means putting them under the magnifying glass because they're interesting and important. You're zooming in and slowing down time.

THE DROPPED COFFEE

Here's an example. In this scene, a character drops a cup of coffee. It could look like this:

> I dropped my coffee on the floor. It was so embarrassing.

But this is an important moment in the story, so the writer magnifies it like this:

> The smell of roasted coffee mingled with bleach and biscuits. I reached out and took the mug. Its smooth sides felt warm. Then pain seared through my fingers and I opened my palm, the handle catching on my index finger. The mug tilted and the fluid flowed like a scalding waterfall in front of me. A starfish formed at my feet as the mug tumbled base over rim towards it.
>
> The crash of china cut through the staffroom, silencing the murmur of conversation. Fragments, some triangular, some strangely curved, the base, round and

perfect, flew in every direction. They bounced off the floor, my shoe, the pedal bin and the cupboard door, rattling and clinking as they span.

My face burned red. I couldn't meet anyone's eye.

In a high-pressure situation, the temptation is to write in a more passive and shallow style, rushing your key scenes, but it's worth taking the time to focus on the minute detail of a moment.

Imagine the scene frozen, broken down into its smallest constituent parts. Focus on each of the senses and try to 'see' the event played out in slow motion in your mind. This works well for action scenes or a moment of revelation or shock.

Check your story for potential scenes. They don't have to be huge fight scenes – they could be as simple as:

- Dropping an ice cream in the sand.
- A football crashing through a window.
- A vehicle collision.
- A wasp sting.
- A chase across a rooftop.
- A wrecking ball demolishing a brick wall.
- The moment a character takes to the stage.
- The pause before an embarrassing conversation.
- Opening a desk drawer, unwrapping a gift or drawing back a shower curtain.
- A gun being fired.

ACTIVITY 49. BOOKENDING YOUR STORY

As we've already pointed out, a well-structured story is a satisfying read. A satisfied reader will buy your next book or, in the case of an exam piece, will give you high marks. Feedback from examination boards often highlights the sophisticated use of structure as a characteristic of good pieces. It shows that you have the audience in mind and are crafting your story, rather than just scribbling out the first ideas that come into your mind.

When you edit, you can consider your opening and your final paragraph. Like an academic essay that argues a point, your introduction and conclusion should be like bookends at either end of your tale. They might mirror each other, they might contradict each other, they might show the 'before' and 'after' of a character. Whatever they do, they should hold your story together.

Think about a film you have recently watched. What was the opening scene? What was the closing scene?

Often, you will find that the opening and closing scenes of a film are the polar opposite of each other. In the Marvel Studios film *Guardians of the Galaxy*, the main character Peter Quill is first shown as a young boy sitting alone in a hospital corridor. His mother is dying. In the final scene, he is surrounded by his new 'family' of friends.

If you can give your opening and closing paragraphs some attention at the end of the writing process, it can make all the difference.

Consider the following:

- Opening scene: A couple holding hands and climbing into the back of a wedding car.

  Closing scene: One member of the couple standing over a shallow grave with a shovel in their hands.

- Opening scene: A beautiful mansion, clad in ivy, birds singing, a car pulling up to the front door.

  Closing scene: A smouldering wreck of a house, roof beams poking out through cracked tiles. No animals stir, all is silent.

ACTIVITY 49

- Opening scene: A man begging on a busy street.

  Closing scene: Same man, dressed in an expensive suit and handing a £20 note to a beggar.

- Opening scene: A woman battling to keep a sailing ship afloat in a storm.

  Closing scene: Same woman sitting by the beach, sipping a cool drink and watching the boats sailing out to sea.

- Opening scene: A busy shopping centre.

  Closing scene: The same place empty and silent apart from a few stumbling zombies.

Now revisit your story. Perhaps there's a way in which you can tidy up the structure. You might want to consider Mirroring (Activity 40).

ACTIVITY 50. KEEP UP THE PACE: THREE VERSIONS OF THE SAME SCENE

The pace of your story is how fast it moves. If it is an action story, lots of things will happen very quickly. Things will change fast. If your story is a description of a beach through the eyes of a pensioner, then maybe fewer things will happen and the change will be slower.

As a rule of thumb, short sentences speed up the pace of the passage, while longer ones slow it down.

Too many long sentences could suck the pace from a scene. Here, a character realises that someone is trying to break into her house, but the long sentences rob the scene of its tension and drama.

VERSION 1:

> Carla gave a short gasp and turned to look at the round, brass door handle. As she watched it, she noticed that it began to turn. It occurred to Carla that maybe someone from outside was trying to get in. She felt really scared and as she backed away from the door, pressing her back against the wall opposite the door, she suddenly realised that there shouldn't have been anyone outside because the house was meant to be empty!

Select a piece you have written in a previous exercise and look through it. Count the number of short and long sentences. Does it work? Is your writing dominated by longer sentences?

If so, the answer is not to go crazy on short sentences. Too many short sentences and you get something that is tiring to read – it stutters and jumps. Here's the scene above again, this time with too many short sentences:

VERSION 2:

> Carla turned. She stared at the door handle. It began to rotate. Somebody was trying to get in. The handle rattled angrily. Carla stumbled back. She pressed herself against the wall. The house was meant to be empty!

Check your work. Is this you? Are too many short sentences creating a stuttering and choppy effect?

Your aim is to introduce variation. Think about a rollercoaster ride. A sudden drop is thrilling and scary but short-lived. Several of these can be exhausting – rather like jump scares in movies. One or two are fine; six or seven and the audience becomes bored.

A classic rollercoaster relies on a combination of slow climbs and sudden, sharp descents. Your story should have a combination of longer, slow-building sentences and short, snappy ones – a little more like this:

VERSION 3:

> Carla turned and stared at the door handle as it began to rotate. Somebody was trying to get in. The handle rattled angrily and Carla stumbled, pressing her back against the wall. The house was meant to be empty!

The sentence length will vary, but if you aim for a long-short-long sentence sandwich or a short-short-long pattern, it will usually work. Try rewriting your piece, or if you want to start afresh, write a short piece using one of the prompts from The Magnified Moment (Activity 48). Give yourself some ground rules that force you to consider sentence length:

- Don't allow yourself more than five words per sentence. Then underline any sentences that don't work in red and any that you would keep in green.

- Don't allow yourself sentences of fewer than five words. Again, underline your successes and failures.

- Then try and rewrite the piece using a variety of sentence lengths.

CHAPTER 7
THE EXAM

FIVE TACTICS TO HELP WITH EXAM PREPARATION

'Sorry, I can't make it tonight. I'm revising for the narrative and descriptive writing question in the English GCSE exam,' said no student ever.

In our experience as teachers, it is almost universally the case that students believe that they don't have to prepare for the creative writing component of the English GCSE exam. It could be about anything – how could they revise for that?

The truth is, they can prepare, and this is how.

We know roughly what kinds of questions will be set in the exam. Students will be shown a picture or given a situation and asked to write about it. It could be getting caught shoplifting, it could be about space travel, it could be about going to a festival or it could be a busy shopping centre.

In a way, it isn't necessary to know any of this in order to be prepared. Students can make up pre-formed characters, images and plot structures, memorise them and then take them into the exam with them. Next time they drink out of a china mug, encourage them to take a quick look at it. It's unlikely to have been handcrafted. If there's an image or logo on it, it probably wasn't painted on individually. In a factory somewhere, thousands of blank mugs rattled off a production line. They were white and unmarked until they went through another process to print the logo onto them. Cars also go through this process. The parts are made all over the world and then shipped to one place to assemble the finished product. The gearbox and steering wheel arrive ready-made. So too does the body of the car, the seats and the windscreen. Everything is prepared somewhere else and brought to the factory.

Your students can plan story components in the same way: imagine the exam is an assembly plant.

Here are the five components they can prepare.

1. OFF-THE-SHELF CHARACTERS

You can make up characters to populate your story before you set foot in the exam hall. They don't have to be completely drawn, but you should have noted down some major details about them. Remember that any characters you create should be flexible. Don't dismiss a plump old woman character just because you've been asked to write about space travel; she's just the kind of unusual character who will make your story interesting. You wouldn't expect an old woman with a knitting habit to be on a dangerous space exploration mission.

- **Appearance**: Think about what your character looks like. Note down three points about their appearance. (*Do not* use the word 'average'!)

- **Wants/needs**: Make a note of what your character wants to achieve in life. You can prepare for this by having two or three wishes: minor ones (e.g. to finish a jumper she is knitting for her granddaughter) through to major or more emotional ones (e.g. to forget the death of her husband or to find acceptance). You don't have to use them all in the story, just one or two.

  Remember: sometimes it's good to visit the 'dark side', and wants and needs are a great place to do this. Your want or need could be quite innocent to begin with but then you can twist it. What if the jumper that the knitting space granny wanted to finish was for a granddaughter who died years before? What if she wants to forget the death of her husband because she murdered him?

- **How might they change?** As we have seen, character change is closely tied to wants and needs. Think about how the character's desires change. Maybe the character realises something about themselves. Maybe the want or need isn't revealed until the end of the story. This creates a twist. Our space granny might not tell the reader that she has killed her husband until the last sentence. This will shock the reader and change their view of the character.

  Character change stories can fit any genre. The granny who killed her husband could be clicking away on her knitting needles in a spaceship or a haunted house. She could be in a romance or sitting on a bus. She could travel back in time or go on a safari.

- **Tics**: Give your character some tics, habits or catchphrases.

■ **Favourite object/item**: Choose something that the character values – something they might go back into a burning building to rescue. The space granny's want or need has provided us with a bag full of wool and some knitting needles. Our dark side idea suggests that she killed her husband with the knitting needles.

■ **Know the different types of character change story**: Is yours a 'lesson learned' story? or a 'fear defeated' story? Get to know the different kinds of character change story and practise sketching them out quickly.

2. READY-MADE MOOD AND IMAGES

Like the characters, you can prefabricate some imagery for your story and memorise it. Again, you may have to adapt some of your ideas once you see the exam question. You shouldn't force something to fit a story when it doesn't really work, but it can cut down your thinking time.

■ **Use the instant pathetic fallacy table to create a few opening sentences**: Learn them. Be prepared to expand them by adding more adjectives.

■ **Learn ten conflict verbs**: Write them down during your planning time, then use them.

■ **Colours and imagery**: Decide on some mood colours and some similes and metaphors to go with them. Write them down and learn them.

3. PRECAST WORLD-BUILDING

It's never wise to try to create a whole world in the short thinking time you have in an exam. Besides, if your world is too complex, or you're too pleased with your invention, you'll spend all your writing time explaining how it works and never tell the story. Remember the tips from Not World-Building (Activity 30) and take some simple worlds in with you!

Revise some major historical events that you could use as a setting. Remember, if you use the *Titanic* as the setting of your story, the reader will know how it will end.

Revise a song, a mode of transport and a fashion item for each decade of the twentieth century and for each quarter of the seventeenth, eighteenth and nineteenth centuries. This is a great way of instantly adding a dash of historical realism to your story.

If you must make up an alien world, come up with three or four details (e.g. sky colour, multiple moons, strange-coloured plants). If you're going to have aliens, make them humanoid or like some kind of creature on Earth; in this way you can describe by comparison.

4. INVERSIONS

Your character may define your story: our space granny harbours a dark secret and she will do anything to stop it getting out. What if someone recognises her? Or she *thinks* that someone does? She might go on a killing spree.

Alternatively, the setting or the question might decide what story you should tell. Either way, it's good to remember some of the other suggestions:

- **Make up some inversions**: This may be a character (e.g. the friendly vampire or the crooked policeman) or a setting (e.g. a horror funfair, a deadly school or a hospital were people are killed).
- **Think up some flaws and challenges**: Again, you may have a character in mind. Give them a weakness and then consider your setting. This may be something you can only do in the exam, but it is worth practising a few different scenarios.

5. POSSIBLE QUESTIONS

Devise your character, then prepare a setting and some images. Use the following table to randomly generate some GCSE exam style writing questions. Use five minutes to plan what you would write and then write for thirty minutes.

Number	Question
1	Write about a time when you were challenged.
2	Write a story set on a crowded beach.
3	Write a story involving time travel.
4	Write the opening part of a story about a place that is severely affected by the weather.
5	Write a story about two people from very different backgrounds.
6	Describe a journey by bus.
7	Write about a time you felt alone.
8	Write a story in which someone breaks the rules.
9	Write a story involving space travel.
10	Describe a train journey.

ACTIVITY 51. THIRTY-NINE WRITING CHALLENGES

Why thirty-nine? Is it because there are normally thirty-nine weeks in a typical school year? Is it like the thirty-nine steps? We don't know!

Like any skill, regular writing practice will improve performance. It will also encourage your students to be brave with their writing and develop a voice of their own. Each challenge in the following table should result in a short piece of around 300 words. Set one of these challenges every week.

Week	Challenge
1	Write a story that starts at the end and uses flashback techniques.
2	Write about a memorable event in your life using the second-person point of view.
3	Write about a kitten playing with a ball of wool but make it sound sinister and disturbing.
4	Write a description of an empty school at night.
5	Write a description of someone using a tool – such as a chef's knife, hammer or drill – without naming it.
6	Write an argument between two people over some kind of belonging, but don't name what it is they are arguing over.
7	Write an account of a squirrel climbing down a tree and along a clothes line to a bird feeder to get some seeds. Make it sound like a heist movie.
8	Write a piece describing a bus journey in which the passenger isn't sure why they are on the bus but slowly realises as they travel.

Week	Challenge
9	Make up four nonsense words for everyday objects. Now write a piece showing what they are by describing characters using them.
10	Describe a bowl of soup in 300 words.
11	Write three diary entries showing three different viewpoints of one event.
12	Write a short story that includes a newspaper, a strawberry jelly and a rusty car exhaust.
13	Three very different people get stuck in a lift. One of them is claustrophobic. Write about what happens.
14	Write a story set in a gym.
15	Write an account of a train journey home from three points of view.
16	Write an inversion of a well-known fairy tale.
17	Imagine a plastic bag being blown down a busy street. Describe its journey.
18	Write a story about a talking cat.
19	Imagine you can't see for some reason. Describe walking through a funfair.
20	Write a description of a supermarket aisle.
21	Describe dropping a china mug of hot coffee on the floor.
22	Write a story involving a secret and a betrayal.

Week	Challenge
23	Write a description of a tree in a storm.
24	Describe a window being smashed by a brick.
25	Write a story in the first-person present tense that involves a wallet.
26	Write a description of walking through a desert landscape.
27	Write a description of a run-down city as seen from the back of a limousine.
28	You come home and a gift-wrapped box is on the kitchen table. Something inside it is moving. Describe the scene as you open it, building the tension.
29	Describe a busy street scene from the point of view of a homeless person sitting in a shop doorway.
30	Write a story that starts where it finishes.
31	Write a story that involves four journeys.
32	Your main character can read minds. What happens?
33	Write a story with a twist set on the *Titanic*.
34	Your narrator is a liar. Write a piece from the viewpoint of an unreliable narrator.
35	Write a story involving three stolen bikes.
36	Describe the front of school at the start of the day.

ACTIVITY 51

Week	Challenge
37	Write a story that involves a cinema ticket, a bus ticket and a parking ticket.
38	Write a description of a storm hitting a city without using the words 'was', 'were', 'would be', 'is', 'will be', 'are', 'am' or any other form of the verb 'to be'.
39	Write a story that starts with a character standing on a motorway bridge.

CONCLUSION

It goes without saying that the activities in this book are not an exhaustive list of ways to encourage creativity in writing, nor are they prescriptive in any way. As a practitioner, you may well be familiar with variants of some of them already and will be eager to adapt new ones to suit your students.

Everything in this book has worked for us at some stage, either as classroom teachers or as visiting authors delivering writing workshops to students aged from seven to seventy.

Creativity isn't a soft subject. It doesn't derive from some divine intervention. It requires professionalism, reflection and constant reiteration to build creative responses. A good, well-structured story doesn't just 'happen'; it is crafted and created with thought, trial and error.

Hopefully, these activities will enable that process. Expecting students to produce a well-crafted piece of creative writing in just forty-five minutes under exam conditions seems to fly in the face of this, but students who have developed their skills in a creative classroom will be able to enter the exam with a head full of 'off-the-shelf' characters, ideas about structure and consistently employed imagery.

It is worth noting, too, that both Martin and Jon brought their writing into the class-room before they were ever published. The teacher-as-writer is a very powerful role model. We don't hesitate to recommend that teachers have a go at these exercises too. You never know where it might lead.

THE *STORYCRAFT* READING AND LISTENING LIST: TWENTY PLACES TO GO NEXT

We're English teachers. Time is tight ... But we're also geekily obsessed by the storytelling process. As a result we thought we'd put together a reading and listening list which allows you to dip quickly in and out during commutes or stolen staffroom moments. Each book or podcast on this list can be consumed in bite-sized chunks and offers huge amounts of indispensable advice and insight. We thoroughly recommend them all. Enjoy!

Fifteen for your eyes:

- James Scott Bell – *Plot and Structure*. Bestselling classic on story shapes.

- Will Gompertz – *Think Like an Artist*. The focus is on fine art, but all the creative principles and approaches are there.

- Christina Hamlett – *Screenwriting for Teens*. Short chapters, simply written, each exploring a basic principle.

- Karl Iglesias – *The 101 Habits of Highly Successful Screenwriters*. Transcripts of writers discussing their craft, arranged by topic.

- Stephen King – *On Writing*. You don't have to love his fiction to take huge amounts from this, particularly the second half.

- Anne Lamont – *Bird by Bird*. Personal stories and observations; a life of writing advice.

- Donald Maass – *Writing 21st Century Fiction*. Punchy, no-nonsense guide to upping stakes and supercharging drama.

- Howard Mittelmark and Sandra Newman – *How NOT to Write a Novel*. Laugh-out-loud parodies of bad narrative writing that teaches as much as it entertains.

- Steven Pressfield – *The War of Art*. The best book written about the stance and attitude of the writer.

- Steven Pressfield – *Turning Pro*. It's *War of Art* part two. Read this one second.

- Blake Snyder – *Save the Cat!* Explores the formula of screenwriting; a genre classic.

- Jerome Stern – *Making Shapely Fiction*. An A–Z of techniques and an excellent section on story types to avoid trying.

- Christopher Vogler – *The Writer's Journey*. Epic deconstruction and discussion of Joseph Campbell's myth-inspired story structure, exploring hundreds of archetypes and tropes.

- Chuck Wendig – *Damn Fine Story*. Funny, light-hearted, clear and helpful.

- John Yorke – *Into the Woods*. Probably the best book on how stories work; superb on structure.

Five for your ears:

- *Geek's Guide to the Galaxy*. For sci-fi and fantasy fans only; many episodes feature interviews with novelists, among the panel discussions about *Star Wars* …

- *The Moment*. Film director Brian Koppelman interviews creatives. Choose the episodes featuring novelists and screenwriters.

- *Scriptnotes*. Two screenwriters, John August and Craig Mazin, dive deep into the nuts and bolts of screenwriting, writing professionally and building story.

- *Story Break*. Irreverent, often hilarious and chaotic attempts to build a story from a title or suggestion. Foul-mouthed and fascinating in equal measure.

- *Writing Excuses*. Ten seasons of discussion, debate and advice in fifteen-minute episodes. Outstanding.

BIBLIOGRAPHY

Bayles, David and Orland, Ted (1993) *Art and Fear: Observations on the Perils (and Rewards) of Artmaking* (New York: Image Continuum).

Bell, James Scott (2005) *Plot and Structure: Techniques and Exercises for Crafting a Plot That Grips Readers from Start to Finish* (Cincinnati, OH: Writer's Digest Books).

Belsky, Scott (2010) *Making Ideas Happen: Overcoming the Obstacles between Vision and Reality* (London: Penguin).

Bransford, Nathan (2010) 'How to Write a One Sentence Pitch', *Nathan Bransford* (20 May). Available at: https://blog.nathanbransford.com/2010/05/how-to-write-one-sentence-pitch.

British Library (2011) *The Writing Life: Authors Speak* [audiobook] (London: British Library Sound Archive).

Brown, Brené (2013) *Daring Greatly: How the Courage to Be Vulnerable Transforms the Way We Live, Love, Parent, and Lead* (London: Penguin).

Corazza, Giovanni (2014) 'Creative Thinking: How to Get Out of the Box and Generate Ideas' [video], *TEDxRoma* (11 March 2014). Available at: https://www.youtube.com/watch?v=bEusrD8g-dM.

Cottrell-Boyce, Frank (2004) *Millions* (London: Macmillan).

Couch, Aaron (2018) 'Tony Gilroy on "Rogue One" Reshoots: They Were in "Terrible Trouble"', *Hollywood Reporter* (5 April). Available at: https://www.hollywoodreporter.com/heat-vision/star-wars-rogue-one-writer-tony-gilroy-opens-up-reshoots-1100060.

Cronin, Matthew and Loewenstein, Jeffrey (2018) *The Craft of Creativity* (Stanford, CA: Stanford Business Books).

Csikszentmihalyi, Mihaly (1997) *Finding Flow: The Psychology of Discovery and Invention* (New York: Harper Perennial).

Department for Education (2012) *Research Evidence on Reading for Pleasure: Education Standards Research Team* (May). Available at: https://assets.publishing.service.gov.uk/government/uploads/system/uploads/attachment_data/file/284286/reading_for_pleasure.pdf.

DiLuzio, Raphael (2012) '7 Steps of Creative Thinking' [video], *TEDxDirigo* (28 June). Available at: https://www.youtube.com/watch?v=MRD-4Tz60KE.

Gardner, Sally (2012) *Maggot Moon* (London: Hot Key Books).

Geirland, John (1996) 'Go with the Flow' [interview with Mihaly Csikszentmihalyi], *Wired* (1 September). Available at: https://www.wired.com/1996/09/czik/.

Godin, Seth (2007) *The Dip: The Extraordinary Benefits of Knowing When to Quit (and When to Stick)* (London: Piatkus).

Godin, Seth (2018) 'No Such Thing (As Writer's Block)' [podcast], *Art19*. Available at: https://art19.com/shows/akimbo/episodes/6e6e4997-65e6-4b77-880f-124da99f05ba.

Gompertz, Will (2015) *Think Like an Artist … and Lead a More Creative, Productive Life* (London: Penguin).

Griffin, Martin (2018) *Payback* (Frome: Chicken House).

Hamlett, Christina (2006) *Screenwriting for Teens: The 100 Principles of Screenwriting Every Budding Writer Must Know* (Studio City, CA: Michael Wiese Productions).

Iglesias, Karl (2011) *The 101 Habits of Highly Successful Screenwriters: Insider Secrets from Hollywood's Top Writers*, 2nd rev. edn (Avon, MA: Adams Media).

Jacobs, William Wymark (1902) 'The Monkey's Paw', in *The Lady of the Barge and Other Stories* (London: Alan Rodgers).

Kelley, Tom and Kelley, David (2014) *Creative Confidence: Unleashing the Creative Potential within Us All* (New York: Crown Business).

Kim, Kyung Hee (2011) 'The Creativity Crisis: The Decrease in Creative Thinking Scores on the Torrance Tests of Creative Thinking', *Creativity Research Journal* 23(4): 285–295.

Kim, Kyung Hee (2015) *The Creativity Challenge: How We Can Recapture American Innovation* (New York: Prometheus Books).

King, Stephen (2000) *On Writing: A Memoir of the Craft* (New York: Simon & Schuster).

King, Stephen (2008) *The Green Mile* (London: Gollancz).

King-Smith, Dick (1983) *The Queen's Nose* (London: Gollancz).

Klein, Gary (2007) 'Performing a Project Premortem', *Harvard Business Review* (September). Available at: https://hbr.org/2007/09/performing-a-project-premortem.

Kleon, Austin (2012) *Steal Like an Artist* (New York: Workman).

Koppelman, Brian (2018) 'The Moment with Brian Koppelman' [interview with Paul Schrader] [podcast], *Stitcher* (22 May). Available at: https://www.stitcher.com/podcast/slate/the-moment-with-brian-koppelman/e/54581735.

Lamar, Cyriaque (2012) 'The 22 Rules of Storytelling, According to Pixar', *io9* (8 June). Available at: https://io9.gizmodo.com/the-22-rules-of-storytelling-according-to-pixar-5916970.

Lamott, Anne (1980) *Bird by Bird: Instructions on Writing and Life* (New York: Anchor Books).

Loewenstein, Jeffrey and Cronin, Matthew (2018) 'Creativity: Think Gourmet Meals, Not Magic Moments', *Psychology Today* (9 May). Available at: https://www.psychologytoday.com/gb/blog/the-craft-creativity/201805/creativity-think-gourmet-meals-not-magic-moments.

Maass, Donald (2012) *Writing 21st Century Fiction: High Impact Techniques for Exceptional Storytelling* (Blue Ash, OH: Writer's Digest Books).

McConnell, Steve (1998) 'The Power of Process'. Available at: https://stevemcconnell.com/articles/the-power-of-process/.

Mayhew, Jon (2012) *The Demon Collector* (London: Bloomsbury Children's Books).

Margolis, Rick (2008) 'A Killer Story: An Interview with Suzanne Collins, Author of *The Hunger Games*', *School Library Journal* (1 September). Available at: https://www.slj.com/?detailStory=a-killer-story-an-interview-with-suzanne-collins-author-of-the-hunger-games.

Michalko, Michael (2001) *Cracking Creativity: The Secrets of Creative Genius* (New York: Ten Speed Press).

Michalko, Michael (2006) *Thinkertoys: A Handbook of Creative-Thinking Techniques*, 2nd edn (New York: Ten Speed Press).

Michalko, Michael (2011) 'Walt Disney's Creative Thinking Technique', *Creative Thinking* (29 August). Available at: http://creativethinking.net/walt-disney%E2%80%99s-creative-thinking-technique/#sthash.EZ4qZMpV.dpbs.

Mittelmark, Howard and Newman, Sandra (2009) *How NOT to Write a Novel: 200 Mistakes to Avoid at All Costs if You Ever Want to Get Published* (London: Penguin).

Naughton, Bill (1968) 'Seventeen Oranges', in *The Goalkeeper's Revenge and Other Stories* (London: Puffin).

Oakes, Steve and Griffin, Martin (2017) *The GCSE Mindset: Activities for Transforming Student Commitment, Motivation and Productivity* (Carmarthen: Crown House Publishing).

Onarheim, Balder (2015) '3 Tools to Become More Creative' [video], *TEDxCopenhagenSalon* (20 January). Available at: https://www.youtube.com/watch?v=g-YScywp6AU.

Pauling, Linus (1961) 'The Genesis of Ideas'. Speech delivered at the Third World Congress of Psychiatry, Montreal, 7 June. Available at http://scarc.library.oregonstate.edu/coll/pauling/calendar/1961/06/7.html#1961s2.7.tei.xml.

Peter, Laurence J. (1977) *Peter's Quotations: Ideas for Our Time* (New York: Bantam Books).

Poehler, Amy (2015) *Yes Please* (London: Picador).

Popova, Maria (2011) 'Scott Belsky on How to Avoid Idea Plateaus', *Brainpickings* (18 March). Available at: https://www.brainpickings.org/2011/03/18/scott-belsky-idea-plateaus/.

Popova, Maria (2012) 'Kurt Vonnegut's 8 Tips on How to Write a Great Story', *Brainpickings* (3 April). Available at: https://www.brainpickings.org/index.php/2012/04/03/kurt-vonnegut-on-writing-stories/.

Pratchett, Terry (2015) 'Notes from a Successful Fantasy Author: Keep It Real', in *A Slip of the Keyboard: Collected Non-Fiction* (London: Corgi).

Pressfield, Steven (2002) *The War of Art: Break Through the Blocks and Win Your Inner Creative Battles* (New York: Black Irish Entertainment).

Pressfield, Steven (2010) *Turning Pro: Tap Your Inner Power and Create Your Life's Work* (New York: Black Irish Entertainment).

Reading Agency (2015) *Literature Review: The Impact of Reading for Pleasure and Empowerment* (June). Available at: https://readingagency.org.uk/news/The%20Impact%20of%20Reading%20for%20Pleasure%20and%20Empowerment.pdf.

Reiss, Steven (2000) *Who Am I? The 16 Basic Desires That Motivate Our Actions and Define Our Personalities* (New York: J.P. Tarcher/Putnam).

Sachar, Louis (2000) *Holes* (London: Bloomsbury).

Seelig, Tina (2012a) 'A Crash Course in Creativity' [video], *TEDxStanford* (1 August). Available at: https://www.youtube.com/watch?v=gyM6rx69iqg.

Seelig, Tina (2012b) *InGenius: A Crash Course on Creativity* (London: Hay House UK).

Snyder, Blake (2005) *Save the Cat! The Last Book on Screenwriting You'll Ever Need* (Studio City, CA: Michael Wiese Productions).

Stern, Jerome (2000) *Making Shapely Fiction* (New York: W.W. Norton).

Usborne, Simon (2017) 'Why Do We Think We're Nicer Than We Actually Are?', *The Guardian* (13 March). Available at: https://www.theguardian.com/science/shortcuts/2017/mar/13/why-do-we-think-were-nicer-than-we-actually-are.

Vogler, Christopher (2007) *The Writer's Journey: Mythic Structure for Writers*, 3rd edn (Studio City, CA: Michael Wiese Productions).

von Oech, Roger (1983) *A Whack on the Side of the Head: How You Can Be More Creative* (Menlo Park, CA: Creative Think).

Vora, Aadil (2015) 'Trick Your Mind into Being Creative' [video], *TEDxNSU* (7 May). Available at: https://www.youtube.com/watch?v=1xWa3Ok2e94.

Wendig, Chuck (2017) *Damn Fine Story: Mastering the Tools of a Powerful Narrative* (Cincinnati, OH: Writer's Digest Books).

Yorke, John (2013) *Into the Woods: How Stories Work and Why We Tell Them* (London: Penguin).

Zacharia, Janine (2015) 'The Bing "Marshmallow Studies": 50 Years of Continuing Research', *Stanford University Bing Nursery School* (24 September). Available at: https://bingschool.stanford.edu/news/bing-marshmallow-studies-50-years-continuing-research.